Advance praise for *Writing to Save Your Life* .

"Everyone has a strong need to have a place in a narrative. With her quick wit, wonderful anecdotes, and great insight, Michele Weldon shows you how to find your place."

—Fern Schumer Chapman
Author, *Motherland*

"Writing to Save Your Life is an invitation to tell the truth. Michele Weldon rolls up her sleeves and encourages her readers to 'open the door,' as she has, and discover the healing power of words. Written with candor, practical application, and plenty of heart, this is a book for veteran and rookie alike."

—Nancy Cobb
Author, *In Lieu of Flowers*

"Clear and compassionate, practical and poetic, Writing to Save Your Life *is the only self-help book you'll ever need. Weldon demonstrates how virtually anything in our lives that confuses, frustrates, or grieves us can be understood—and overcome—by putting words on paper. This book, for both men and women, is as optimistic and affirming as any I've read."*

—Neil Chethik
Author, *FatherLoss*

Praise for Michele Weldon and *I Closed My Eyes* . . .

"[Michele] Weldon has built her career by writing—sometimes in explicit detail—about her own life. . . . No matter what the topic she comes across as strong, funny, and frank."
—Chicago Magazine

"[Michele] Weldon is an intelligent, self-confident, talented journalist. . . . During a time when memoirs are the hot ticket to publication, Weldon's is written better than most and carries a strong message."
—Booklist

"Whenever I see [Michele] Weldon's byline above a magazine or newspaper article, I know I'm in for a good read. She delivers bright, introspective pieces without being stuffy or preachy."
—Chicago Sun-Times

A "potent and painfully honest chronicle."
—Atlanta Journal-Constitution

"Writing has always been her refuge. Little did she know it would become her salvation."
—Oak Park (Ill.) Pioneer Press

"Finely honed prose [that is] uplifting and self-affirming."
—Library Journal

Michele Weldon "unabashedly exposes her emotions and keenly analyzes past events that add depth to her story."
—Chicago Tribune

"A gripping, personal story."
—Publishers Weekly

Writing to Save Your Life

How to Honor Your Story
Through Journaling

MICHELE WELDON

HAZELDEN®

Hazelden
Center City, Minnesota 55012-0176

1-800-328-0094
1-651-213-4590 (Fax)
www.hazelden.org

Library of Congress Cataloging-in-Publication Data
Weldon, Michele, 1958-
    Writing to save your life : how to honor your story through journaling / Michele Weldon.
        p. cm.
    Includes bibliographical references.
    ISBN 1-56838-742-3 (pbk.)
        1. Diaries–Therapeutic use. 2. Diaries–Authorship. 3. Autobiographical memory. I.
Title.

RC489.D5 .W455 2001
615.8'516–dc21   2001024803

05 04 03 02 01   6 5 4 3 2 1

Cover design by Mary Brucken
Interior design by Terri Kinne
Typesetting by Terry Webster

To Weldon, Brendan, and Colin,

for who they are and who they will become

contents

Part 1: Preparing for the Journey

Part 2: Paving the Road with Your Words

Foreword

by Pamela Holtzman, R.N., L.C.S.W.,
and Stuart Pinkwater, Psy.D.

The discipline of writing empowers us to creatively express who we are. By challenging ourselves to be honest and put our voices on paper, we cannot help but disrupt old patterns and beliefs. We all have the capacities for growth, change, and adaptation, but we often lack opportunity for their expression. Writing is a portrayal of our personal experiences, a tool to enhance understanding and gain perspective.

In *Writing to Save Your Life*, Michele Weldon shows us how to use writing to heal mind, body, and spirit. She is passionate in her beliefs and respectful of the human spirit. Through her generous use of stories, she encourages us to turn ourselves inside out, while writing it all down.

Prodding us to pick up the pen and go to it, Weldon directs us down our own paths. With a compassionate sense of humor and unrelenting encouragement, she gives permission to spill out everything, from the painful to the mundane. Her exercises help us dig down into ourselves and mine our own truths. An enthusiastic cheerleader, Weldon uses *Writing to Save Your Life* as a guide to help us tell our own stories, to write it down and save our own lives.

Our minds defend us and trick us. Our bodies carry emotions and feelings, whether we recognize them or not. In our workshops at The Write Path, we utilize techniques of meditation and journaling. We encourage people to discover and express themselves without the filter of criticism that inevitably edits memories and experiences. Writing is a way to sort through painful remembrances, let go of them, and be delivered from them. Meditation and visualization allow us to soften, listen with kindness, witness even the most painful stories without judgment. When we become quiet inside, we remove the self-consciousness that fogs our access to the truth. We gain clarity.

Pamela Holtzman, R.N., L.C.S.W., has a private clinical practice in Buffalo Grove, Illinois. She is cofounder of The Write Path and presenter of Compassionate Fatigue workshops. Her background includes an education that is both medical and psychosocial. Fifteen years of clinical experience as a hospice nurse as well as psychotherapist is the foundation of her body-mind-spirit approach.

Stuart Pinkwater, Psy.D., is a clinical psychologist and an educator. He is the coordinator of family services at the Cancer Wellness Center in Northbrook, Illinois. He created the Writing for Health program at the center and has used writing as a therapeutic tool in his private practice. He is also the cofounder of The Write Path, a series of workshops that uses meditation and writing as means of self-exploration.

Acknowledgments

I am exceptionally grateful to Clay Garner for suggesting I try a book on writing and for believing in my work and my ideas. My editor Corrine Casanova worked carefully to smooth all the rough parts of the book to make it cohesive and whole. Anne Hawkins, my agent, is witty and intuitive, knew what I envisioned, and helped me to see how to do it. Particularly helpful in jump-starting the process of this book was my former college roommate Laney Katz Becker, who introduced me to Anne.

My sisters, Mary Pat, Maureen, and Madeleine, are wise and nurturing and offer me a foundation to do everything I dream. My mother provides unconditional support for everything I write and dare to do. My brothers, Bill and Paul, are not only unfathomably funny and encouraging but also admirable sources of strength for me and my three boys, Weldon, Brendan, and Colin, who are not only my inspiration in writing but also my sustenance. My sisters-in-law, Bernadette and Madonna, are always kind and believe in who I am and who I aim to be. My brother-in-law Ken offers his assistance for the boys and me, while Mike is boundlessly generous with his time and his heart. I am endlessly appreciative. And I am profoundly grateful for the enduring legacy of love from my father, Papa Bill, who I know is always with me.

It is because of my closest friends that I feel I can dance out on a limb and still feel connected and safe. Ellen Schofield remains a stalwart ally, while Laurel Davis listens and understands my life. My dear friend Maxine Ellman helps me to calm down so I can grow. Lisa Lauren is forever ready to make me laugh. There will always be Dana Halsted, no matter how far away we live from each other, with whom I have a bond that does not falter. Linda Berger urges me with intelligent sensitivity to keep striving as a writer, a mother, and a friend. Lillian Flowers helped me to heal with her words and nudges me where I need to go.

At Northwestern University's Medill School of Journalism, my colleagues Jon Ziomek, Stephan Garnett, David Nelson, and Susan Figliulio push me to challenge myself to succeed. Cassandra West, my editor at "WOMANEWS" in the *Chicago Tribune*, not only offers a space for my work but consistently gives me an opportunity to interview fascinating, creative people. Denise Joyce, my editor at the "Health and Family" section of the *Chicago Tribune*, also allows me the luxury of having my voice heard by so many. Several of the essays appearing in this book were first published in the *Chicago Tribune*. Chuck Cozette, my editor at *West Suburban Living* magazine, where some essays in this book were printed for the first time, affords me a chance to regularly write what makes me laugh and what makes me wonder.

The men and women in my Writing to Save Your Life workshops help me to articulate my passions about writing and coax me into becoming a better writer with their observations and lessons. The undergraduate and graduate students in my classes at Northwestern are exceptionally bright, and so full of enthusiasm and light that they keep me charged and engaged. From those who have come to my book signings, speeches, and events, I have received more than I could ever give back. To those hundreds of readers who have written me tender and hopeful letters, I am profoundly appreciative for their gentle words that lend me permission to keep writing.

There are many others who contribute to my life and fill me with laughter and comfort. Because of their gracious support, I am able to write. And because I write, I can save my life.

I thank you all.

Introduction

Giving Sorrow Words

We are all natural storytellers.

From the imaginative stories we tell as children about ghosts and fairies, princes and dragons to the simple conversations we may have with a close friend at the end of the day, we instinctively know how to articulate the details of our lives. But sometimes the stories that matter most, the secrets we hold inside, the events and emotions that have shaped us more than we can admit at times are what we are reluctant to release and put into words.

But it is just that act that is freeing.

"Give sorrow words," William Shakespeare wrote in *Macbeth*. In the centuries before and after his simple call to pen, many thousands of authors, poets, playwrights, journalists, and essayists have used their own words to tell stories that help them heal through crisis; that console them in grief, loss, pain, challenge, or growth; that celebrate the joy in their lives.

Now it is your turn.

Writing heals. Offering illumination and a path to closure, writing is more than simply placing words on paper. Done honestly, writing acknowledges who we are and what affects us. Without honoring the past in our own words with our own uncensored reflections, our memories threaten to dry up and wither away until they are lost.

A good friend of mine, Miriam, lost her beloved husband suddenly in January 1999 when he had a fatal heart attack on a business trip, leaving her to raise their two little boys alone. Her pain led her to writing, which she did for comfort and catharsis. Months after the late-night phone call from a hospital nurse telling her he had "expired," she wrote, "Tomorrow lingered in my head and became a weight so heavy I felt as if I were drowning. . . . How do I save my children when I am free-falling into an abyss with no bottom in sight?"

But Miriam told me that going back to the writing regularly to help her deal with these feelings also aided her in seeing how far she had come in the healing. With the second anniversary of her husband's death only days away, she said she would go back and write to reexamine her feelings and see how much she has changed.

The writing helped her to start healing.

Writing Heals

The therapy of writing is not only medicine for the soul but also a microscope to analyze intellectually and creatively your role in the world and your reactions and insights to whatever it is you need to tell. The writing can serve as the beginning of a longer, more profound evolution.

"One writes in order to feel," Muriel Rukeyser wrote in her 1949 book, *The Life of Poetry*.

Stepping back to look at your life is similar to looking at a large lake—or even at an ocean from a beach. When you look at the water, you see it as blue, then you can notice the striations of turquoise, darker blue, and bluish green the farther out you look. You see it all swirling together, the colors merging into a flow that is hard to define. But when you bend down at the water's edge, scoop the water in your hands, and let it fall through your fingers, it seems clear. When you scoop up the details of your life, hold them in your hands and write, they seem clear.

Clarity is a crucial step toward celebration. Clarity places what Frank McCourt, author of best-sellers *Angela's Ashes* and *'Tis*, calls "the ingredients of a life" into context. You can take the separate elements that create your history and place them together in words. Writing down your life and examining your words offers perspective. You can literally see what your past means to you by reading the words you have ascribed to your experiences. You can closely examine your own story. Now on paper, your experience has body, weight, and substance. You have offered your story meaning.

"We all write to tell our stories, I suppose," McCourt said in his lilting brogue on a windy October evening in the Dominican University auditorium filled with devoted fans of his two memoirs. "I spent all those years in the classroom, when mostly what I wanted to do was write," said McCourt, who taught high school for thirty years in New York. Later, in a private reception with champagne and canapés of phyllo dough with crispy shrimp and wheels of soft cheese, I waited in a polite line of supporters anxiously clutching his books for an autograph.

When I reached the front of the line, he stood up and shook my hand gently. I asked him whether he thought writing saved his life. "I would have been incomplete, dissatisfied, and floundering around if not for that," he said as I scribbled his comments into a notebook. "Writing serves its purpose for me and gives me such satisfaction that just to have it printed would have been enough."

His celebrity as a result of his words was not the true worth of his work. For him, the celebration was the writing and the naming of his childhood for what it was—the truth he could lend to his own history.

Writing has the potential to heal anyone and everyone who commits to the process, not only creative professional writers whose words are their livelihood and whose published works help others to understand themselves. Without the ominous prospect of publishing your story, without the fear of anyone reading your work to criticize, blame, or burn you in effigy, writing the truth helps you to explore the past and move beyond it.

"My function as a writer," wrote Laura Riding Jackson in the 1935 book *Progress of Stories*, "is not story-telling, but truth-telling, to make things plain."

This book is about the process—making the truth plain for yourself—not the end result of publishing a work. This book is not just about the exercise of writing, though you will stretch that muscle. This book is not aimed at augmenting your creativity or your gratitude, though that may naturally happen. This book is about the writing as work, as joy, as a tool to complete a specific task: healing.

You are here in these pages, I hope, because you know what story it is you need to tell. Or if you have not named it yet, you are shadowed by thoughts, feelings, memories, and emotions that you are aware you need to express. You feel compelled to write and driven to try writing as a way out of the cave. This book will help you to do that.

"For me writing something down was the only road out," author Anne Tyler wrote in 1980.

Though I am a journalist and author, my goal is not to guide you to a writing career, though I wish you well and hope it happens if that is your choice. My goal is to help you in the process of writing and to make the process itself joyful and healing. The prize arrives in the act of writing, not by having others read the finished work. And I know the process will help you.

A Practical Guide to Your Journey

In this book, every chapter offers a new concept and approach to each stage of writing. I have designed exercises in each chapter to help you attain each goal and move you on in your mission of healing in your own words. It's a pragmatic approach to guide and give you some concrete instruction on which to hang your hat. The exercises can take several minutes or they can take several hours. You can do one exercise at a time or pick one that you think will be most helpful. You can read the book first without the exercises, then go back and do the exercises later.

Ideally, you will do all of the exercises in the book and use them to help you write your truth. I suggest you answer the questions in writing, because if you respond orally, you are choosing not to give your words physical space. When you do commit your words to paper, they have a different, more concrete and less ephemeral power. They simply last longer. And you can reread what you have written.

I believe in the show-don't-tell school of writing. Each group of exercises is followed by an essay I have written, with an explanation of what I was dealing with in my life at the time and how my writing helped me understand myself and the world around me. Many of these essays have been published in the *Chicago Tribune*, others in magazines such as *West Suburban Living* where I write a column in each issue, and still others are new essays published here for the first time.

I included the essays in this book not only to show you how the process works but also to reveal more of my own truth. Perhaps they will make you laugh. Perhaps you will feel understood when you read them, knowing something similar has happened to you. Perhaps my writing will help you by example. Perhaps the essays will prompt your own memories or offer you a device or technique that you will want to use in your own writing.

Tools Needed to Jump-Start Your Writing

The first half of the book, "Preparing for the Journey," eases you into the writing work and prepares the way for the healing to come from your own words. It is preparation of the foundation of your work. The second half of the book, "Paving the Road with Your Words," gives you tools to construct the road to healing and be the engineer of your own healing script. You can revisit the second half of the book over and over with each new subject you want to explore.

To begin, all you need is a space to write. It can be a permanent part of your home, a favorite desk and chair, or a laptop computer you take with you on the train, in airports, or to bed late at night. It is immaterial whether you type on a personal computer or an old typewriter, or write with pencil, pen, or quill and ink. I have some wonderful pens I have been given by thoughtful friends, but I tend to lose them, just as I lose sunglasses. I find that it is not the pen or the paper that matters, but what I write.

You can write on lined legal paper, a memo pad, or even in a journal stored in your nightstand. You can set up your writing area as a haven with a fine wood desk, an elaborate desk set, and Italian paper that is smooth and exquisite. You can buy paperweights you love to hold. You can have an inspiring quote over your desk that may help you focus. On the wall over my computer desk is a framed quote in black calligraphy on a lavender poster. It is by Jorge Luis Borges and it reads: "Writing is nothing more than a guided dream."

It's What Inside That Counts

But the tools are not as important as what is in your heart and what will come through in your words. You decide the what and when. I will help you with the why and how.

You may choose to type your story using an elaborate font and complete the package with a designer cover. You may keep your writing in a drawer now, but plan to transfer it all into a bound leather blank book with black pages using a special white-ink pen. You may put your work in a clear plastic cover with a binding so you can place it on a bookshelf and know it is saved forever. But know that how you treat your words is significant. You want to be able to look back on this process and celebrate your words, so do what is right for you.

Preserve your words any way you see fit. If you feel you just have to get it out first—on napkins grabbed at restaurants, on the backs of bank deposit slips or laundry receipts—and worry about how you will assemble it all later, fine. But do not lose your words. Keep them in a safe place, in a special drawer, a file cabinet at work, or a box in the kitchen, so you can celebrate them now and later for the courage it took to transform feelings and thoughts into physical representation.

But commit to the writing and do the work.

"You must do the thing you think you cannot do," Eleanor Roosevelt once said. You may not have considered writing forbidden such as a child considers drawing on the walls with crayons or markers. But you may have thought of writing about your own life as an intimidating, daunting proposal. You may have contemplated the stories of your life but dismissed writing them down as too difficult or painful. You may have even thought it was egotistical or not worth the effort.

It is not egotistical. It is worth the effort. You can do this.

This Can Be Fun

You need to use your words to save your life. "Saving your life" has two meanings: rescue or salvation, and preservation of your own truth. While so many have an image of writers as dark souls avoiding food and company while swatting the bats of brooding thoughts, the big secret and the good news is that writing can be fun.

Writing can be an enjoyable physical endeavor, just as gardening, cooking, or washing a car can be. It involves all of your intelligence and ingenuity and calls on you to be present for the task. When you plant your spring garden, you are digging and pulling with your hands in the dirt, thinking what goes where and why, picturing the blooming results. When you cook a festive meal, you are using your hands to measure, knead, stir, and chop, thinking about timing, taste, and presentation. Even when you clean your car, vacuum the backseat, and empty the bins and ashtrays, your work is deliberate and thorough so your car will look and feel better to you.

When you write, you are using your hands as instruments of your heart and mind. You may find yourself smiling as you uncover forgotten details. You may marvel in the way you place words together to form a phrase that explains precisely what you mean and expresses exactly what it felt like at a certain moment, painting a scene for you that is vivid and real. And like a beautiful garden, a clean car, or a delicious meal, the end result will reflect the work, skill, and time you spent doing it.

"Use your words," I have told my three sons since they were each toddlers. It was a way I had learned to try to soften their behavior toward each other, to get them to listen first before acting out. It was an alternative for them instead of using their fists or feet to make a point; a tool of a phrase employed to stop fights, tantrums, retaliation, or even just a day's end outburst of screaming or crying. But it wasn't until I used my own words about my life that I could see how profound that simple directive was. Use your words to listen to what is inside of you.

Scribotherapy: A Therapeutic Tool

Using your words is what I call scribotherapy. Like bibliotherapy, which is defined in *Webster's Third New International Dictionary* as the "guidance in the solution of personal problems through directed reading," scribotherapy is a word and regimen I created and assign to the process of using words as a conduit to understanding and feeling relief from any life difficulty.

I am not a medical doctor, psychologist, therapist, social worker, researcher, scientist, sociologist, or psychiatrist. I am not qualified to tell you scientifically how and why your spirit, body, and soul will be healed by writing.

I am not qualified to tell you the psychological justifications for the claim that writing heals.

I can only tell you it does work.

I am a mother, author, university lecturer, workshop instructor, public speaker, advocate, volunteer, daughter, sister, and friend. I am a person just like you, with aches, sighs, and laughter in my heart, struggling to make sense of it all and lead a joyful life with a goal of making the lives of those around me simpler and better. I can tell you the truth: Writing has helped to save my life.

I am not a great writer—though my writing feels great to me—nor am I likely to be considered one of the great writers of my time. But my words have served me well, shaped my outlook, and served to calm me, as yours can serve you.

"Writing is a kind of double living," historian and essayist Catherine Drinker Bowen wrote in 1957 in *The Atlantic* magazine. "The writer experiences everything twice. Once in reality and once in that mirror which waits always before or behind."

Telling an Important Story in Your Words

As a professional journalist for more than twenty years, I used the tools of reporting to uncover truths of the thousands of people I have written about in newspapers and magazines. But it wasn't until I used those tools to tell my own story that I began to see the true worth of my training. It wasn't until then that my own words could help to heal me. It wasn't until then that my words were much more than a means to a paycheck or the building blocks of a career. My words were my own salvation. Our words become a prayer, a song, a poem, a narrative of who we are, where we have been, and where we wish to be.

There are scores of instructive and enlightening books on writing that have helped me to grow as a writer and as a person (see the "Recommended Reading" section). But most of the books I have read over the years speak to me as a professional writer. They have helped me in the sales of my stories and books and in my struggle to improve at my craft.

Some of the other books I've read approach writing as if it were a hobby such as needlepoint or decoupage and assert that what you choose to write about is arbitrary. Some books deal with writing as if it were some brand of drive-by creativity, as if writing about mashed potatoes can be as meaningful to you as writing about your grandmother's death and how it changed everything for you and your family.

Writing is not like that for me, and I wager if you have a story to tell, it is not like that for you. What I write about chooses me. I know what kinds of things I want to explore in writing and they are always with me, perhaps in the back of my mind, sometimes buried deep, but they are with me. Just as my children are always with me, what I want and need to write about is with me persistently. I know what it is I need to explore for resolution, comfort, relief, and release.

This book will not help you write around the periphery of your life as an arbitrary pumping of your creative juices, but write specifically to save your life and preserve your story.

I am not here to help you sell your memoir or assure you that your life will be immortalized along with the works of other stellar memoirists such as Frank McCourt, Anne Lamott, Kathryn Harrison, Annie Dillard, or Rick Bragg. I am here to help you excavate your own truth and articulate your own story in a way that is meaningful so that you can grow and heal from your experiences. I will do my best to help you move beyond a superficial retelling of events to saving your life in a way that is fulfilling for you. I will do my best to guide you to the center of it all so you can write about it with heart. I will show you what worked for me.

What I promise you is this: I will offer you the tools I provide my university journalism students as well as those men and women in my Writing to Save Your Life workshops. These are the tools I use. The promise I make is not that your life will become completely different, though you may experience that. I can't promise you will look different or suddenly have wittier friends. I can't promise that what has been bothering you, the stone in your shoe that perhaps has begun to feel like a boulder, will be tossed aside for good.

What I promise is to tell you all that I know about how to shrink the pebble in my shoe and have the truth loosen its grip on my neck so I can breathe easier and live better. Writing does that for me. To me, writing is about washing yourself clean of dishonesty until truth shakes free like pebbles from the beach caught in the cuffs of your pants.

There is evidence beyond my experience that suggests writing can help.

Writing as Therapy

A recent study in *The Journal of the American Medical Association* shows that patients suffering with illnesses from asthma to rheumatoid arthritis experience less pain overall when they write during stressful periods. The North Dakota State University psychiatrist conducting the study claimed by spending one hour writing daily, those patients who wrote about their feelings improved their physical conditions and reduced their reports of ailments by 50 percent.

I am not saying writing is a miracle panacea or suggesting you will be healthier and stronger as a result. I am suggesting that by writing you can begin to heal, whether that healing manifests itself in reduced physical symptoms or simply a shift in attitude. You may only feel lighter, calmer, or happier as a result. It may be small. It may be everything.

Whether you are looking for an outlet because of an illness, life change, work issue, loss, or other event, you will find by putting your experiences into words that you grow from the process in a positive way. You also can save a life that is joyful and full of gifts you wish to acknowledge and pay tribute to in your own words. Whatever your motivation, writing can help.

"Writing forces consciousness," Melody Beattie wrote in *The Lessons of Love*.

Writing is a salve that can help you recuperate and reclaim your life along with a larger repertoire of professional and personal support. You may want to seek individual or group therapy as avenues to help you face and understand the stories you hold inside. To seek counseling of others is not to admit

to access your strength because you are willing to confront

a healthy, contemplative life. Whatever you choose, know

ill help by itself or in concert with further professional, social,

port.

Writing helped me recover from divorce, rebuild my life, regain strength, and move past the pain. As a parent of three boys, it helps me in trying to understand who they are and how I can better serve them with love, respect, and understanding. It helps me as a friend to analyze my relationships: those I cherish and those I know I need to release. Writing helps me to understand my own family: my mother, my brothers and sisters, and how the death of my father changed me and my view of the world.

Easing me toward forgiveness, writing mellows my resistance the way a good friend can nudge you to try a roller-coaster ride for the first time or watch a scary movie you would never dare see alone. And that you ultimately enjoy. Your words can keep you company, holding your hand. Words can be the companion and the solution to your fear.

Author Alice Walker calls for the need to "witness" in her work and tell stories of her life and the lives of other people. For me, writing is witnessing my own life. Writing feels safe to me, a refuge from the burning, the water to douse the flame and extinguish the pain.

Writing is calming to me, though the maelstrom of feelings provoked from writing sometimes appears to do just the opposite. But I have come to think of writing as unclogging the kitchen sink. Unless you poke through what is stopping it from flowing, the water will sit, stagnant, eventually backing up and spilling all over the floor. At some point, it starts to smell and everyone who walks in your kitchen takes a few conspicuous sniffs.

Daring to Deal with It

You eventually have to deal with it. When you deal with what is there, you may get your hands dirty, but you can pull up the muck and face it. Writing about the muck, you can see what the problem is. You can hold the words on paper in your hands, put them down if you can't bear to read them, but know they are there if you dare to. You can uncover your story and let the rest of your life flow around where the muck was. And you can take a good, long, hard look at what caused all that smell in the first place.

With my first book, *I Closed My Eyes*, I tried to heal myself by writing about my marriage and explain to myself how I got into that relationship, how I got out, and how I eventually started to get better and experience joy again.

After the book was published in 1999, I started offering Writing to Save Your Life workshops because I had answered so many questions informally about writing. I thought this would be an appropriate avenue. The workshops have been enormously rewarding. At each session, I learn something original and surprising from my students that energizes me. I also learn that all of us have something to face, some clog in our sinks that we need to clean out. Even if what is there is good and useful, we want to be able to see it up close in our writing.

Rarely does someone come to my workshop without having a conviction about what he or she needed to write. Sometimes the clog is really a triumph, masquerading as blockage until you look at it, write about it, and learn where it belongs in your life.

Taking the Plunge

It is my wish with this book to help anyone who cares to take a chance on writing to deal with an event, issue, or recurrent emotion. This is for all of us who want to look at ourselves honestly and use writing as a way to heal, as a pathway to uncovering our spirituality and our wisdom. Writing is not intended to replace living your life, or to keep you stuck in the past. Writing is the spotlight on your life, the flashlight on your helmet to keep you moving through the tunnel, illuminated.

If this is a new way for you, I thank you for taking the chance to discover your truth and heal. If you are already writing, I thank you for trusting me to be able to tell you something new and useful. It is a way to find what has been lost. It is a way to reclaim yourself.

By writing this book, I am using my words to articulate my passions and sincere beliefs about writing; it is healing me further and filling me up, offering me clarity, solace, and justification for my life's work. So I thank you for participating in my continued journey.

At the start of each chapter, I use the words of my students, workshop participants, friends, and readers who have written me their stories to serve as inspiration and illumination. I chose words from men and women who are not world-famous writers. I made that choice to illustrate that writing is accessible to all of us. It is not an elusive craft limited to those who excel professionally.

Anyone who writes can heal from the process.

A former graduate student of mine, Sumiko was an extremely bright young woman, who was mostly quiet during class discussions, though her laugh was infectious and her enthusiasm and talent huge. On the last day of class, I asked each student what they can take from the class and use in their lives.

"I learned that this is not just about writing stories," Sumiko offered. "Writing is a pathway to discover yourself."

Amen.

Part One

Preparing for the Journey

chapter 1

Writing Is Talking on Paper:

Working through Procrastination and Fear

I know now I can get started and take one step at a time. It's OK that every-thing doesn't pour out of me perfectly on the first draft. I'm ready to access and acknowledge my own experiences in a more open way than before.

—Rachel, Writing to Save Your Life Workshop participant

Stop Procrastinating and Just Write It Down

I tell my students that I know they want to have written more than they want to write. No matter whether I give my students five or ten weeks for a large assignment, invariably a few hysterical students will call the night before it is due, sometimes at 11:00 P.M., and ask me to explain the assignment more fully, wanting advice on what they can do now because ohmygod it's due in the morning. They are panicked and feel worse than if they would just do it—if they would just trust the process and their own talents.

Just as Nike has urged us to just do it for years, you need to stop procrasti-nating and do the writing. Just write it down. I tell my students that learning to live with deadlines, even self-imposed ones, is not a bad way to live your life. In everything you do, you do your best work in the time allowed. And then you move on. Write today, then move on to tomorrow.

Procrastinators don't get a lot of writing done.

Your story will stay locked inside of you unless you write. No more excuses. Write it down.

In one writing workshop, I offered a brief spontaneous writing assignment, and one of the women was clearly displeased. She was frowning and fidgeting in her seat, while all the others were writing madly and engrossed in their work. After the exercise was over, about fifteen minutes later, I asked each one to offer how they felt before, during, and after the exercise. I was secretly hoping she would pass on sharing her comments as I was afraid of what she would say.

"I hated it," she said. "I didn't know we would have to write in this class," she explained. "I thought you would just talk about writing."

You can't just talk about the work, you have to do it. We all have friends and acquaintances who are one day going to get another job, paint the living room, or in-line skate to the beach. We are all going to clean the basement, lose weight, get a new job, call old friends, and live happily ever after. If only there were more time, if only I were in the mood, if only the weather were better, if only my children were older and less needy. If only anything. If only everything.

Making the Commitment

If only you had the time to write.

If only is there—only if we choose it to be. You cannot heal by reading about writing to heal, though you can begin to believe in the possibility of healing that way. But you cannot save your life in your own words unless you write those words. It is the writing that will save your life. Not the thinking about writing or the wanting your writing to save your life. It is the writing. No more excuses.

"Making a decision to write was a lot like deciding to jump into a frozen lake," Maya Angelou wrote in *The Heart of a Woman*.

But do go ahead and jump.

Years ago I heard an author speak at a book signing and say that before she wrote her book, she ironed all the guest towels in her house. The next week she alphabetized her spices in the spice rack. Finally, weeks into her self-imposed delay, with her deadline hovering over her head like a police helicopter, she had an immaculate home organized from CDs to shampoos. Now she felt free to start.

I remember thinking how silly that was, but that was years before I tried to write an honest book and understood what she was doing. In my first book, I wrote the beginning and the end and made each a lot longer because it was far too difficult emotionally to face the middle. Eventually I stopped the delays and wrote what I needed to. And I did feel better.

I was writing around the truth, but my procrastination was as real as if I spent my time organizing the videotapes thematically to have a mini-Blockbuster store in the basement.

Don't iron the guest towels. Don't alphabetize the spices. Don't organize the videotapes. Write.

"There's no perfect time to write," wrote prolific best-selling author Barbara Kingsolver in *Writer's Digest* magazine in 1994. She wrote *The Poisonwood Bible* and *Prodigal Summer*. "There's only now."

Writing is just talking on paper. If you believe that simple concept and if you tell yourself that writing is only talking to yourself, you can eliminate the first five hundred excuses for not writing. If you want to write, then write. You can't get better and you can't get to the heart of your truth until you pay homage to the words inside you and write them down.

Still, I understand the drive not to write. Sometimes, if I am getting ready to write a difficult essay, I play a game with myself and allow myself a treat, a physical jump start for my brain with new scenery or companionship. I tell myself I will go for a walk in the morning with a friend or I will run out to a favorite local boutique and just look, just get ideas, just get turned on creatively. And then I'll start with no excuses.

I have learned that I can only do this if I set limits and give myself a deadline. If I don't, my treat can eat up a good part of my day. Unless I set a limit of thirty to forty-five minutes, my summertime walks with my friend Laurel can stretch an hour or more when I really need to go home and start writing. By then, I rationalize that I need a shower. Then of course, I have to dry my hair.

Then I have to figure out what I am going to wear that day and try on ten "goal" outfits in the back of my closet. These goal outfits are ones that are a little too tight now but that I can wear when I drop a few pounds and get in better shape. I need to check to see whether they can all fit after my hour walk.

The Avoidance Factor

I won't even talk about the mail syndrome of going through the newly arrived mail a few times a day to make sure you don't miss the deadline on the coupons or the new releases at Blockbuster. Catalogs should be recycled without so much as a peek. You don't need to order new blinds today. You need to write. I've heard all the excuses; I've done them all. Writing has a much higher return on your sanity than checking the models' catalog photographs for obvious signs of retouching.

You can tell yourself you need to clear your head all day, all week, all summer. But unless you begin to write, you can't justify clearing out all the closets and drawers and giving all your family's outgrown clothes to the veterans group. You can't make a case for spot cleaning the furniture and replacing the knobs on the kitchen cabinets (I ran out to buy the silver-toned ones in the shapes of spoons, knives, and forks). You can't justify reading all your children's papers since kindergarten or organizing the photos in the photo album for the last fifteen holidays.

You can make any task more worthwhile than your writing, but you must realize it isn't. And you won't begin to heal and save your life unless you write.

There is a boutique on Oak Park Avenue, a few miles from my house, that I love. It has unique clothes, sweaters, jackets, and dresses. It also has very unusual home accessories, jewelry, and candles. I walk in there and automatically feel better; the store always smells good from the bath soaps, candles, and sprays.

I guess I didn't realize how much I walked in there to feel better until recently. There was a furniture throw that I had been admiring for several months. It is a tawny and bronze Aubusson-style throw in linen and velvet that would look great in my living room on the cantaloupe-colored couch. It was large enough and long enough that I could lie on the couch and read to

Brendan and Colin with us all wrapped in it, cozy and soft. I loved it.

Each time I was in the store, I would admire it, pull it out from the stack of throws, feel it, look at the price tag of $160, and wonder how I could ever afford it. And each time I asked the salesclerk when it would go on sale. The last time I was in there was the day before my birthday. I had an essay due for the *Chicago Tribune* later that day and gave myself an hour to run errands, copy articles at the print store, and window-shop for inspiration.

"Will this ever go on sale?" I asked the clerk yet again.

The clerk was matter-of-fact. "No, if it doesn't sell here soon, we will send it to one of our other stores." She paused and added politely, "But you should really think about buying it for yourself because it would save you the time of having to visit it."

I guess I looked as surprised as if I had been discovered with my hand in the cookie jar.

"You always come in here and admire it," she continued, now clearly afraid that she had offended a customer with her honesty. "If it was in your home, it would save you the time and energy of having to come here to be with it."

I bought the throw. After all, it was almost my birthday.

Sometimes you have to stop visiting your ideas. Write them down, validate your ideas in your own words. Write instead of shopping, write instead of watching the 10:00 P.M. news. Write on the train once a week instead of reading a magazine. Grocery shop on-line and get back to the writing. Write instead of flipping through new magazines, even the ones with the latest news on who's wearing what. Write to feel your life and live in the present. Don't put off the writing. When you have an idea, validate your own creativity and honor it by writing it down.

Confronting the Fear Head-On

Jump the hurdle of inertia and write. But then don't place another hurdle in front of your writing: the fear of being judged. The fear of writing because you will be misheard is a blue whale–size excuse for not writing. Bonnie Friedman wrote in her book *Writing Past Dark*, "When I embraced imperfection, silence dissolved."

Let the silence of your wordlessness dissolve like salt in water.

The fear of being judged as hypersensitive or alarmist is another excuse for not writing. You are telling yourself you only have this one thing to write about, and it really isn't anything big, you should just get some rest and get over it. You don't really need to heal from it; it's nothing. It's not an ear infection and it's not pneumonia. Get over it.

But I know you have a truth you need to tell. I hear you. Ignore the busy doctor or the critic in your head who may look like Sister Mary Josephine in the third grade or the poetry professor you had in college with the suede elbow patches on his tweed blazer talking about why your poetry is so unimportant.

No one will judge you here. No one will tell you it is really nothing and send you home to another sleepless night. I encourage you. I know you need to do this. You are not writing this for anyone but yourself. So let yourself be heard by you.

Truth and Privacy: It's Your Own Words

Your words are not primed for publication and will not be e-mailed, faxed, or sent to another soul unless you choose that to happen. Because you have taken the step to write down the words and claim what is inside you, it does not mean you will be driving down the expressway tomorrow and see your words on a billboard.

They are still *your words*. It is still your truth. The act of writing your thoughts and feelings does not relinquish the property rights to your past. You have sole custody of all of it. Releasing the words from inside you does not loosen your control of the words and their truth. It only loosens the power the pain has on you. You are reclaiming the truth and proclaiming it. You don't need any audience other than yourself. You will feel good, like when you take off your shoes after a long day. Write it down. It feels better.

Your story will not be a front-page exposé on the cover of a supermarket tabloid. You will not be placing your paper towels, pain reliever, and extension cord on the black rubber conveyor in the checkout line at Target and glance over to see your words in sixty-point type on a magazine cover with the worst imaginable photo of you in a bathing suit. This simply will not happen. This only happens to royals, actors, and presidential interns, and then only if what they have done is simply outrageous.

The ironic part is you may be afraid of telling when you really should be afraid of *not* telling. Containing the truth is risky. Keeping it all subverted and shoved inside has the power to make you more fearful and keep you halted. Like carbon monoxide, it has the power to poison the air silently and slowly. That is until you write it down, put your feelings on paper, and take the power back. Until you testify. Even if you testify only to yourself on a yellow legal pad, you have sworn the truth is nothing but the truth.

"Good writing is about telling the truth," novelist and memoirist Anne Lamott wrote in her bible of good writing, *Bird by Bird*. It's a book I quote from so often to my classes that several of my Northwestern graduate students one summer gave me a beautiful, graceful silver bracelet with the inscription "bird by bird."

The writing will be good because it is true. Own that belief. Your story is yours and you have taken control of it. Once acknowledged in words, the truth can be put in perspective and will relinquish its stranglehold on you. You'll be free.

Exercises

1. Start the process by identifying your fears. Simply make a list answering these questions: What are you afraid of? Is it causing you to procrastinate? Write down what scares you about writing the truth. Is it because you fear someone will find out or are unsure how you will feel when you begin to write? Is it because you are afraid you can't say it perfectly or it won't help? Answering honestly may help you dispel some of these notions.

2. Now read the list and separate the fears that come from you and those that come from others. The fears you generate can be "I don't know how to

write this" or "It won't be good enough" or whatever comes into your mind that could stop you. Next to each one of these fears, write, "I will write anyway." To answer those fears that are coming from outside of you, such as a fear of criticism, write the same: "I will write anyway."

3. Write down the possibilities of your fears coming true. Can you dispel them? Is there something you can do to ensure your writing stays private? Can you set up a support system in advance of your writing so you have someone to go to when you feel vulnerable? If you are afraid you can't write well, know that you are the perfect person to tell your story—you're the only one who can. No one can tell it better than you. Trust yourself and trust your words.

4. Have a plan. Write down specifically what you will do when you feel afraid of what you are about to write or what you have written. Can you call a close friend, a therapist, or a clergymember? Can you practice calming your fears with a reassuring mantra such as "I own my words and I own my story"? Tell yourself that you will do your best and it is good enough. It is all you need to do. It is perfect.

In this essay, I wrote about my fears as a parent. Fear can paralyze you and keep you from writing. It can be the reason you procrastinate; it can be behind your inertia. Writing about what you are afraid of can free you. The *Chicago Tribune* ran this essay in the "Health and Family" section in January 2001. As a parent, I have many fears fueled by events in my backyard and in the world. I explored many of them here. Writing about the fears helped me to face why I was so scared much of the time, legitimizing them as well as putting them in perspective.

Like you, I have fears about my writing and fears about telling the truth. But it is the telling and the writing that keep my fears at bay and strengthen me. Try to face the fears in your words. They will seem smaller and less terrifying.

Everything to Fear Including Fear Itself

E. coli lurks on my kitchen counters and in the nearly indiscernible puffs of pink inside the hamburgers I grill. Bogeymen skulk past the school playground and stalk my children from the Internet. The fourth-grader who teases my middle son will retrieve his father's gun and bring it to school to show his friends.

What am I afraid of? What am I not afraid of? With three boys in my charge, you name it, and I have fantasized, imagined, and worried about it.

Luckily I am years past the infant and toddler phases when parental phobias threatened to consume me. I heeded all those warnings in the parenting books about choking on hot dogs, peanuts, and peas. Still, having placed all my babies confidently on their stomachs to sleep as their pediatrician recommended back then, I learned after my youngest was out of a crib that it was the worst possible thing I could have done.

Thankfully no infant with my DNA rolled off a bed or slipped too often in the tub, though my oldest at age two once took my car keys from my purse, ran to the only electrical outlet in an empty gymnasium, and tried to "start it." I screeched and rescued. My boys have had stitches (Brendan has had twenty-three) and a triage nurse's collection of bruises, bumps, skids, and cuts from a variety of heretofore unpredicted encounters with tables, stairs, doors, bicycles, swing sets, and Rollerblades. Though no one has broken a bone, I am not out of the woods yet. I am terrified of puberty.

They will be bigger than me. They will drive. Ohmygoodness. They will date. There will be basements involved and lots of their friends all down there together and nobody having to be home until midnight. There will be proms. There will be shaving. There will be R-rated movies. They will get home from school before I get home from work. They will be much bigger than me.

As a paranoid journalist and parent (a worrisome combination), I read the newspapers and magazines, watch the TV news and news magazine shows, and mostly come away with something new to fear for my children. What I do with all this horrifying input is not live my life as a crazed harpy trying to prevent life from happening to my boys, though I could see that as one possibility. No. I live my life as a parent knowing in the nucleus of each maternal cell that I can't truly protect them from anything.

Regardless of the graphic and gory projections I can conjure (at any second of every day), I know I can only do so much. Short of stocking up a cabin in far northern Wisconsin with a few years' worth of beef jerky, juice boxes, and E-rated Nintendo games, I can't save the children. Besides, there would probably be bears near the cabin. If I had to homeschool all three boys, I wager the boys would prefer to take their chances with the bears.

"Fear is the beginning of wisdom," Eugénie de Guérin wrote in 1838. Perhaps she was on to something. As the youngest of six, I never believed parenthood would be a delirious joyride from playpen to Sears Portrait Studio to kindergarten to college and back to the portrait studio. Growing up I knew of children who were killed in car accidents and others who drowned in shallow lakes outside their summer homes. While I never felt my children were doomed, I always felt there was a lot in their lives I could not control. Perhaps that is the true wisdom.

I shoulder the onerous task of their care solemnly, considering it my gift, having these serendipitous, tender lives under my watch. I knew from the first drip of the epidural before my oldest son, Weldon, was born that I would do everything in my power to tease from life any joy I could for them, attempting all the while to avoid disasters, man-made or natural. But what really shakes the freckles off my arms is that as a parent I may not be able to stop any of the bad things from happening, no matter how many vitamins, swimming lessons, or well-fitting shoes they have.

As much as I want to guarantee each of them a life without pain or even mild inconvenience, I realize I am ultimately powerless. That is the starter drive, the igniting spark of my fear.

One Sunday last winter, in the clean aftermath of a blizzard, I brought the boys to a sledding hill at a local college's outdoor field. After an hour or so, we were collecting ourselves to leave, blessedly without injury or frostbite. Colin was in his sled he calls "the rocket," and as I knelt down to pick up a glove, the rope slipped from me and he went racing down the side of the hill, headed for a pile of twenty-foot steel pipes precariously perched off to the side.

As I ran after him screaming, I was simultaneously cursing myself and praying for a miracle. His sled careened into the pipes and he spilled crying onto the frozen snow, like a bag of Yukon Gold baking potatoes that had spilled from the bottom of the grocery cart. I scooped him up and started to cry, imagining his head cut and bleeding inside his ski cap.

I felt his head and neck gingerly, quickly pulled off his cap. And I cried more from relief. He was fine. It's funny, but I was never afraid of sledding before.

As a parent I find that I usually trade in familiar fears for new ones, like playing a card game of Go Fish. The pile grows, the pile shrinks, big fears exchanged for smaller ones. Each night when I look back over the day, I am grateful for what has come into our lives and also for what hasn't. I celebrate the dreams that come true. And I rejoice in the fears that don't.

chapter 2

Igniting Your Power

I want to go home and write.

—Mary, Writing to Save Your Life Workshop participant

Following Your Dreams

Unless you count my brief childhood delusion thinking I would grow up to be a prima ballerina floating across the stage in a filmy, pale pink tutu on the *Ed Sullivan Show*, I have wanted to be a writer for as long as I can remember.

When I was ten years old, I inherited my sister Madeleine's publishing empire. She had founded and developed the *Juvenile Journal*, a monthly publication of typed news of family, neighborhood, and occasional world events that she copied on a desktop machine called a hectograph my father bought her for the endeavor.

The *Juvenile Journal* press operation took place in the second-floor sunroom off my brother Paul's room. The bare bones of the empire sat on a large wooden desk facing two walls of windows. Once a month, when the briefcase-size machine was pulled out from under Madeleine's bed for production, the metal stand with four suction cups was placed on the desk and became the whole print-shop enterprise.

The machine had a yellow, gelled surface where I placed the freshly typed carbons (the messy, blue-black, oily paper that smeared on your hands and your clothes and was positioned behind every white sheet of paper as Madeleine or I typed). The process is long since outdated but known to every typist, secretary, journalist, author, and teacher who worked before the dawn of Xerox and dry photocopying.

After removing the carbons and wetting the gel with a small kitchen sponge, I added clean white sheets of paper on the surface, pulling them back after pressing them hard with a marble paperweight and rubbing to get as dark an imprint of the typed lines of words as possible. I pulled off each copy, slightly damp and curled, and laid them to dry on the floor.

The smell from copying reminded me of a dentist office or a mixture of glue and paint. It filled the room with a sense of hard work and productivity. The result was bright purple copies to be assembled and stapled later, after dinner, but before my brothers or sisters would push them aside. Each issue had four to six pages of what I was sure was brilliant, unforgettable, purple prose.

I apprenticed with Madeleine for several issues, but my first solo issue after Madeleine discovered boys and the art of being a teenager was in August 1968. The issue was a chronicle of my family's trip to California that summer. The first article was about our arrival in San Francisco, something I considered as monumental as a presidential parade complete with several visiting heads of state.

"The four hour plane ride was fun," I wrote. "We could see Chicago as a small blob. After a while we arrived at the hotel where we drove to our room via a ramp. After resting we tried to make a 3:30 P.M. cruise. We rushed to Fisherman's Wharf, arrived at 3:25, got in a huge line. The wrong line! Tragedy!!! We were very disappointed, but then we saw a cable car. . . . By the way, we saw 62 hippies today."

This was the beginning of my writing life. Each month I exposed such fascinating news as family meals, birthdays, and school events and on occasion would editorialize, with illustrations, about popular fashion or current events. Like my sister before me, I abandoned my publishing empire in high school when I also discovered boys. I was certainly no longer willing to be associated with anything dubbed juvenile.

Confidence Is the Key

When the *Juvenile Journal* folded, I was astonished to learn that I was theoretically deeply in debt. Were it not for my father, who mailed each issue to the thirty or so subscribers (most of them relatives and my mother's bridge-club friends) without charging me for postage, paper, hectograph machine, or typewriter, I could not have sent my first issue. But he did support me in every way possible. It was the foundation and validation for all my writing since. It helped me see power in my words.

I never felt ridiculed, doubted, or second-guessed. If I wanted to run a monthly newspaper out of the second-floor sunroom, fine. My father would keep mailing out my issues as long as I would keep typing and copying them. My mother would keep persuading her friends to subscribe at 50¢ a year. And she would keep saving the issues in her bottom dresser drawer where she kept her delicate ribbon-knit suits and the fragile evening bags I loved to touch.

I wrote poetry in high school and college and kept a journal all through my twenties. I learned early that writing was my way of dealing with the world, a way I found that was free from worry and the regular preteen insecurity about what anyone else thought about everything I did. I could worry for days about what to wear to the Friday night dance at the local boys high school, but I never worried whether anyone would like what I wrote. Even if I did sit in Mr. Baker's Latin class diagramming my outfits for the week so there would be no repeats (purple vest, white blouse, pink bell-bottoms on Monday), the writing part of me was not as cautious, insecure, or fearful.

I kept the writing me separate from the me that crumbled if another girl said she disliked my eye shadow or shoes or asked what I did to my hair. For some reason, I dared to write about other subjects besides myself. My writing was immune from the social paranoia that swirled around me every other moment of the day. I wrote simply because I liked to.

That is a lesson I still embrace.

Exposing the Truth

In twenty years of writing, the help I sought always came from the writing, not from the publication. You will feel the impact of your writing without ever showing it to another soul. Without the threat of being naked all the time to the world, you can reap the benefits of your own self-exposure.

You need to ignite your power and permit yourself to tell the truth, the real truth, the sometimes ugly truth. It is that truth that holds your power. Like Dorothy in *The Wizard of Oz* you had the power to go home all along. You were capable of getting back to Kansas on your own volition, you just needed Glinda, the Good Witch, to tell you how.

Click your heels three times. I will be your Glinda.

The power is yours. Claim it. Claim your commitment to writing. Write to save your life because your life is worth saving. And if you are weary of telling yourself that, let me tell you—please listen to me. Your life is worth saving. You need to write down what it is you need to deal with, heal from, celebrate, or inspect.

Your life is worth remembering, immortalizing. Your feelings need to be saved. Write them down.

When I was growing up, there was a series of commercials for Fruit of the Loom underwear that preceded the funny guys dressed in the oversized fruit costumes of the cornucopia logo. In these commercials, there was a tough, mean, lunch lady of a woman with a snarl and a hiss who inspected men's briefs coming off the assembly line. In a comic gesture of exaggeration, she snarled as she pulled and stretched and held the seams up to the light. Only when she was satisfied that they were up to quality standards would she place her "inspected by" approval stamp on the plastic bag of men's white briefs.

Think of yourself as your own life's inspector. You owe it to yourself to inspect what story you are carrying inside of you. Look at it, stretch it, monitor the seams. You can't inspect it unless you have something to hold in your hands. You have to write it down to really look at it.

Hold the words in your hands. Turn on your power.

And write.

Exercises

1. Make a list of your writing goals. Do you want to enjoy the process? Do you hope to learn more about yourself or the events in your life? Will you learn what happened by explaining it to yourself in words? Is it something from the recent past or your childhood that you want to explain? Do you want to challenge yourself creatively by trying to explain something specific, such as the reason you dislike organized sports or why you spend a lot of time alone? Do you simply want to get the truth about your past out so you can look at it?

2. Write down why writing makes you feel powerful. Is it the unique way you put words together? Is it because you tell the truth? Because your work is private? Are you proud of the way you write? Do your words have an energy on paper that allows you to feel, think, and understand something or someone better?

3. Write down this phrase: My words have power. Say that several times before you begin to write. After you have finished a writing exercise, say it again. Realize that the power of your words is coming from you.

This essay is an example of taking one part of your life and writing about it to understand it. Is there some habit you have or way you act that you want to write about? Is there something about your life you can examine in your own words as a way to see how you bartered on your power or put obstacles in the way of looking at your truth?

I was teased by a fair number of friends about how many pillows I had in my house. You could call me Pillow Woman. I wrote to discover for myself why I had been making those pillows diligently all those years—as a form of denial, a form of procrastination, a way to avoid my own truth and the power of that truth.

Pillows were my excuse for not facing myself and igniting my own power. I spent years with eyes closed, sewing up my truth in beautiful bundles that insulated and protected me from confronting what was happening in my own home. You certainly could never tell by looking at my heaps of colorful and meticulously fashioned pillow treasures that my home was a dangerous place for me physically, emotionally, and spiritually. In this essay I explored my reasons for making those pillows and how they kept me busy and distracted from the truth I needed to tell myself, the truth I eventually found the courage to write down.

Don't make pillows instead of writing. Don't be so afraid of what you will find that you refuse to look. When you decide you need to save your life in your own words, then write. And stop manufacturing the excuses. I know because I was an excuse pillow factory.

We all have our pillows. Yours may be shoes or sports, but something is keeping you from telling yourself the truth. Something is occupying your writing time. Understand what it is and let it go. Sew the last pillow and sit down to write down the truth.

A Cushioned Life:
Hiding behind the Pillows to Avoid the Truth

The surgeon at Evanston Hospital advised me to rest as much as possible for at least one week, maybe two or three. He told me to be careful not to lift anything heavy, lest I undo the stitches where my appendix used to be. Of course, I couldn't work. The prospect of two weeks alone, trapped and immobile without deadlines, scared me. I was twenty-three and the kind of woman who thrived on frenzy, the kind of woman who needed crowds around her to feel safe. If I were too silent for too long, I just might have to look at myself.

It was an unwelcome temporary retirement. In my Lincoln Park studio apartment a few blocks from Lake Michigan and the zoo I loved to stroll to on Saturdays, I started sewing pillows by hand. I watched TV and sewed pillows. At first I made a pair of pillows for my bed in a tawny chintz with grand, gesturing leaves and tangles of exotic flowers. I had shuffled slowly to the fabric store a few blocks away and pushed through the bolts of fabric until I found a bolt that suited me. I labored back to my apartment with a yard of the crisp, polished cotton.

Projects always made me feel worthwhile, whether they were relationships, articles, dinners, watercolor paintings, or new jobs with bosses I needed to wow. Over the next few weeks, I hand stitched a half-dozen pillows, some in vibrant, jewel-toned silk to add drama to my oatmeal-colored cotton couch. Others were in a brooding, Oriental print to throw on a dark red reclining chair that was too large and cumbersome for the space, but a gift from an old boyfriend whose memory I was not yet ready to discard completely.

I liked the clumsy, comfortable chair even if it was always in the way when I had parties and someone trying to dance invariably tripped over it. It had an ottoman that obstructed the view of the twenty-one-inch color TV I had bought and charged on my Marshall Field's account because I had had no money in my checking account to pay for it. A woman needs a TV.

It was a small apartment, where in one sweeping glance I could see all that I owned. If I strained my neck, I could inventory my walk-in closet where I shoved the oversized walnut dresser, the one from my mother's old bedroom set, the one with the mirror now stained dark from age in corner streaks of gray and black spots.

The full-size bed was pushed beneath one of the two windows facing Wrightwood Avenue. Near the radiator that hissed and clanged in the winter was the cream writing desk with the fussy gold trim my mother gave me—reluctantly—when I moved to my first apartment.

My boyfriend Dan had helped move my things, and my mother clearly disliked him and all that he meant. He was a photographer, gregarious and worldly, and she cringed with every pot and pan he lifted and placed in the rented trailer. He chattered nonstop. My father appeared indifferent to him, as if he was transparent and inconsequential, as if he knew that in a matter of months he would be gone from my life, the photographs of us fading in a drawer. My father never really seemed to see the men I was with, the ones at the dinner table on holidays. He saw past them, as I always did.

Against the wall where I heard my neighbors fighting was the Haitian cotton sofa, the one that every unmarried person in the late seventies owned: contemporary, simple, blockish, like a bus seat. On the couch, I placed the gold, royal blue, and fuchsia pillows I had sewn. I didn't like my pillows to match; I didn't like me to match, not my shoes to my purse, not my jacket to my skirt, not my life to my dreams. I thought it made me more interesting at parties.

In front of the couch was the wood-and-glass coffee table I bought for $60 at one of those bare-bones discount stores with the furniture piled high and haphazardly in front of the windows. On either side of the sofa were two ceramic elephants painted cobalt blue. On each elephant's back I placed a circle of tabletop glass. Now they were end tables. My mother had given me two matching Waterford lamps with cream silk shades, so I placed them on the elephants and laughed at how grand they looked in the midst of all this economy. The lamps probably cost more than the couch, bed, and chair combined.

I loved this apartment because it was mine alone. I had no roommate and no pets. I cared for it meticulously, lovingly, cleaning its nooks, surfaces, and corners every Saturday morning without fail, unlike most of my friends who would clean only if they expected company or their mother to drop by. The pine-cleaner bottle would last me six months with just a few splashes on a paper towel to complete a weekly job. I could vacuum the entire apartment without unplugging the cord. It was a testament, I thought, to a well-edited, contained life.

The colors of the next pillows I made were warm hues of browns and golds, brick reds and honeys, with the occasional jewel tone for whimsy. I had written a story about a color consultant back then, and she told me with a straight face that I was an "autumn." I took this diagnosis to heart. I believed in labels then and felt if you only surrendered to the natural order of things and played out your season in all you do, then your life would make sense. I wore brown and beige and imagined life was easy.

Following a few promotions and raises at the trade magazine where I worked, I moved into a bigger apartment on Cedar Street two years later and began dating the man I later married. I brought my handmade pillows with me, but I stopped sewing new ones and gave myself little time for my own creativity. We moved to Dallas three years later.

I started making pillows again, first in my two-bedroom apartment in a red-brick complex with a swimming pool that was always crowded. I had free time so I made white eyelet pillows for my bed and more chintz pillows for the couch in the spare bedroom where my sisters slept when they came to visit, where I slept when my parents came to visit.

Later, after we were married, my husband told me the pillows were too feminine and in the way whenever he wanted to lie down. We had moved to a duplex on Oram Street, where the couple upstairs, we later learned, heard every word said or shouted. I re-covered the Haitian cotton couch in white silk with a white-on-white paisley pattern that seemed art deco and exotic to me. I changed the brightly toned pillows to the Southwest tones of soft turquoise, pale pink, and sun-washed yellow.

I made more white pillows for the bed we bought at an antique sale, and he wood-stained the bed a honey tone. "This looks like a woman's room," he said curtly, out of the blue. I thought it had been a good day. When we went to bed at night, he took the pillows I had made by hand and finished with cording and tassels, and threw them all on the floor.

In 1988, when I was pregnant with our first son, the doctor ordered me on bed rest for the last two months because of toxemia. I sewed more pillows than I had before. I would retire to bed, with my swelling feet elevated. I would sew something for the nursery, which was only a nook between the dining room and the kitchen, but which seemed magical to me and miraculous because a little human—my human—would reside there.

For the wicker chair beneath the window, I sewed white cotton pillows with pastel trim filled with trains and bunnies. I made a black-and-white-checkered bunny with batting inside for his crib. *If I could just plan enough and make the room perfect, everything will be fine,* I thought. Make enough pillows and make enough plans.

We left Dallas when Weldon was ten weeks old and moved to Indiana, where my husband started law school. At first we lived in the house where my family spent the summers. It was a red-brick Georgian on Lake Michigan—bus stop 22 on Lake Shore Drive in Long Beach, Indiana—and the lake was frozen solid white as far as you could see. It seemed as if you were looking at the surface of the moon, with its craters of ice and peaks of snow. It was just as isolating.

The sky seemed gray all winter and sometimes the horizon was hard to distinguish. You couldn't always tell where the sky began or the ice ended. I didn't know where I began or ended. My father had been dead a year and he had never known his seventeenth grand-child. My husband was in law school and home little, but the edges of our life had inexplicably been whittled sharp and I was so tired. There was a sadness about me I could not articulate, a hollowness growing wider and deeper, but I was exhausted and overwhelmed and tried not to think about anything too long or too hard. Even with a small child who slept little and whose erratic rhythms I strained to assimilate, I made more pillows.

That summer we moved to a small, stone ranch house closer to campus. I set out to make more pillows than ever, convinced I need-ed to transform this small space into the home that would make us happy ever after. It was a house perched on an acre of untamed grass, bushes, weeds, and, we later learned, poison ivy. We painted all the walls white and replaced old, stained carpeting with new, beige plush carpeting. I retiled the bathroom floor and made curtains for every room. I was alone most of the time with our oldest son, soon expecting a second. I had no close friends. I bought oversized metal numerals at the hardware store and nailed them to the front door—1219—so we would never miss a delivery or visiting friends. I wanted to be sure I was found there because I felt so lost.

Every week I would drive to the nearby mall and walk through the aisles of the one fabric store: planning, comparing, pretending that if I bought one yard of fabric and made the perfect pillow for that one space, then our home would be happy. I had enough spare money for one yard of fabric. One more pillow and it would all be OK.

I sewed many pillows in three and a half years, filling up the family room, living room, our room, and the boys' bedrooms with every coordinating swatch of cotton I could find. Some pillows had one fabric on the front and a different fabric on the back, and I could turn them over on whim to make the room look different. Some I hand painted with fabric paints. I counted once and had made forty-six. I recovered some more than once, many more than twice.

I made twenty-three pillows for the living room alone. I bought rich brocades and sewed them in neat squares and tied them with silk cords like packages. I would do anything to pretend I was someone else with someone else's life for the few hours it took to create a pillow: picking out the thread, paying close attention with each hand stitch. For two hours, I could be someone else; I didn't have to be me. Two hours I didn't have to see the truth.

I had coffee one winter afternoon at the rented house of a woman I had met, a friendship I was desperate to cultivate to sweeten the acid taste of my loneliness. I was always thirsty for someone to talk to, someone who could see me, someone who could hear what I wouldn't say out loud. It was a drowning thirst, with my mouth so thick and parched I felt I could never drink enough to be satisfied.

She was also the wife of a law student and had a small child like I did. Brendan and Weldon crawled or ran across the bare wood floor of the old kitchen where she made pasta almost every night of the week. We talked about our husbands, our babies, our lives before, law loans, and being lonely. I was afraid to hint at anything more complicated, more true, afraid what I was hiding would scare her away. And then I would have no one.

I wouldn't have thought it possible, but she had even more pillows in her house than me, plus baskets of stacked pillows perched on the floor. I hadn't even thought of placing pillows in baskets. She said she sewed them at night when she was alone so she wouldn't go crazy. Sometimes she and I took our babies and went to the movies in the middle of the day and stood in the back of the theater, rocking them on our hips if they cried. We seemed to understand each other. So many of the days seemed bleak. So many of the nights seemed worse.

I get Christmas cards from her still. She has four children that she is homeschooling and was expecting twins. She was shocked by the news of my divorce and sent me lines from the Bible for encouragement, each scripted in swirling, synchronized swimming kind of loops. She appears to be a woman with all the time in the world. Sometimes in her letters she talks about the decorating she has done. Her husband's career is galloping forward.

When I knew her, she was exceptionally beautiful with long, auburn hair framing a heart-shaped face. She was tall and lean and wore long cotton skirts she made herself, the kind that wrapped around her like an apron and tied at the waist. We both owned the same pair of fisherman sandals in brown leather that each of us had bought—in different states, no less—years before we met each other. It made us laugh.

It's been almost a decade since law school graduation and I

don't know what she looks like anymore; she sends pictures of the children. I wonder whether she still has time for pillows.

We moved back to Chicago in 1992 after graduation with two boys under three into a 3,000-square-foot Tudor home with a mortgage bigger than it probably should have been. But this house would be the answer to my prayers and any price was worth it.

I made the boys cowboy pillows with ropes tied in lassos. I painted black splotches on white cotton pillows to make them look like cowhide. I sewed red-and-white gingham square pillows to decorate the radiator top and made pillows from large silk scarves so the boys could lie on the floor with blankets in the family room and watch TV. I made sailor pillows, zoo pillows, pillows zooming with cars and trucks. Their room had fourteen pillows by the time I was finished, and the family room had twelve.

I felt that if I went to bed after finishing a pillow I was all right; my family was insulated. I was trying to make my life more comfortable, more cushioned, safe. When I was making pillows, I was in control and could be someone other than someone's wife, someone's mother, anonymous, unworthy, hurt. Back then I had a hard time relaxing. I was afraid of what I would see if I were still.

Each pillow required skill and patience, and if I concentrated, I could make something beautiful at the end of the night no matter how dangerous the day had been, how hurtful. I could change the face of a room with a yard of fabric and three yards of fringe, even if it was my life that needed to change instead.

I needed the pillows to keep me from feeling hurt and to distract me from feeling at all. To keep me from focusing on what I needed to see. I craved the comfort those pillows promised. I gave them as gifts to myself when no one else could comfort me, when I refused to comfort myself in a way that was real and not just an effort at duplicating what I saw in a home-decorating magazine. If my home looked happy, we would be happy.

The day after the divorce was finalized more than five years ago,

I put that house up for sale. It was more than a year before it sold, and I had moved with the boys to a house a few miles away.

I haven't made pillows in years.

I tell myself it's because I haven't had time. But I don't think, even if I were to have the time, that I would choose again to make another pillow, and certainly not the dozens and dozens of pillows I needed then to distract me from my life. I don't need them anymore to cushion my fall. I am not planning on ever making a free fall like that again. I made pillows so I didn't have to look at my life, the man I married, or who I became. I made pillows so I didn't have to write about the truth, so I could hurt less. I made pillows to muffle the screams from my soul, so our house was a padded cell I hoped could silence the chaos within, could silence me, could keep absorbing the tears.

I made pillows so no one would know. I made pillows so no one could hear. I made pillows so I would not feel.

I could never have made enough. So I stopped.

chapter 3

Focus on the Big Idea

I need to write to gain courage.

—Alice, Writing to Save Your Life Workshop participant

Removing the Clutter

A young woman with cropped brown hair and a great laugh came to a workshop I offered one spring and confessed she had too many ideas so she couldn't write at all. This was her excuse for staying immobilized. She said she didn't know where to begin because she was a bubbling hot spring of ideas. She said her brain was crowded. That's an original excuse: You have so many things in your life worth saving, you can't possibly choose where to begin. So you can't save any of it. It all gets lost.

The other participants in the workshop did not warm to this declaration, mainly because a more frequent complaint from those daring to write is that they don't know where to begin on their one idea. They just know the writing will make them better. More often an excuse for not writing is the blankness of the page, not an overflow of the brain.

But I told this young woman that, though it may feel as if she has one thousand ideas in her head, the truth is she has about ten. It's just that she won't let them out so they keep bumping into each other. Her ideas are acting like balls in a pinball game, bouncing against each other and clanging, ding-ing, and alarming her with messages that they need to be noticed. But she needs to pick one at a time. She needs to pick one idea and focus on it. Make it the Big Idea. Form it carefully and completely as a single sentence and set to working on it without further ado. Once you name the Big Idea, the healing can begin.

For this woman in the workshop, her ideas had become like a Saturday morning of errands. You know how that goes: You wake up with a start, panic that you have to go here, pick up that, drop this person off, have this finished by Monday, and make yourself crazy by letting it all bump around in your head like pinballs. Without a list, you can drive all over town all day and still not make it to the bank before it closes.

Until you write it down and see that all you really have to do is go to the cleaners, the grocery store, and a basketball game, you feel completely over-whelmed and put upon, drowning in requirements for your time, anxious and resentful. But writing it down helps you see that you can do it all. You can do what you need to get done. One idea at a time.

By writing down the ideas that are swimming in your head, it's as if you are letting the turtles out of the terrarium. The funny thing about turtles is they will all sleep on top of each other no matter what size the terrarium. They are probably wishing in their green little turtle brains that it wasn't so crowded in this silly place and that they could have a rock of their own to sleep on. But they are making it crowded by choice. You can't think clearly and set your ideas free unless you open the door and write them down.

Then you can pick the Big Idea where you want to start today.

Tackling the Big Idea

Having a working list allows you to be able to whittle down to the Big Idea. The Big Idea is the story that needs to be told first; it is the little boy in the sec-ond grade with his arm waving madly, begging to be called on by the teacher, squealing in pain. "Ooo, ooo, ooo, I know, I know, I know! Call on me, ooo, ooo, ooo, ooo, ooo!" Call on the one Big Idea that screams for your attention.

Your Big Idea is a permission slip to tackle one story at a time. You can suspend the urgency of the other stories in your head and concentrate on one Big Idea at a time. You will know what you need to write first because the deep stories, the stories you need to heal from, are the apple-sized dustballs under your bed or your dresser that you have hidden and can no longer ignore—the ones that will clog your vacuum or choke the cat.

Your Big Idea is that looming, messy dustball that lets you know it's there. I tell my Northwestern University students as well as my workshop students that you need to have your Big Idea fully formed before you write a sentence.

Focus, Focus

"What's the Big Idea?" It's a cartoon phrase Bugs Bunny would say indignantly to Daffy Duck before he spits a response. Make it simple, make your Big Idea one declarative sentence, a bumper sticker claiming your truth. And keep the bumper sticker with you as you write.

You don't want your bumper sticker to read "My life stinks," even if you think that to be a very succinct and clever phrase, worthy of permanent adherence to the back of your car. You want to be as specific as possible to be able to articulate exactly what you need to heal.

For instance, your bumper sticker could be "My mother was not there for me when I was young" or "I didn't get the job I loved." If you make your truth too broad, such as "Life is unfair" or "I am sad," you could write for a hundred years and never get to exactly what is troubling you.

Without a Big Idea, you could write around the problem and not experience the relief and healing I suggest. It's like when you are on a diet—which if you're like me, has been for the last twenty-seven years—and you start to think about a large order of french fries. But of course, you can't have french fries, so instead you make yourself have an apple, or some yogurt, but you're still hungry. So you eat some crackers—maybe with just a smidgen of onion dip—and later, a banana.

Then you pour yourself a Diet Coke with lots of ice, thinking maybe your mouth just wants to be busy. You end up heating up a bowl of soup, followed by a glass of juice, more crackers, this time with a little peanut butter, and maybe a bowl of unbuttered popcorn.

Now you're stuffed.

Trust me, you will eat more if you eat around your craving then if you just went ahead and ordered a small fries in a mad dash to the drive-through.

The same holds true for shopping around a craving for something new. If you see a $40 shirt on sale and tell yourself you can't afford it, instead of working it out with yourself, fidgeting with your budget and saving for it, you will buy around it, treating yourself to a scarf, maybe shoes, or a new pair of sunglasses at $20 each. You always end up spending more.

The point is don't write around the truth. Find the Big Idea and stick to it.

Make the Big Idea perfectly state what you mean to say. This is the bumper sticker, the declaration of what it is you need to heal. You know instinctively the story you need to tell yourself in writing. You know what you need to put down on paper. This may be the first time you have ever dared to let the truth out, and just seeing the words in ink may scare you. I understand. It is scary. It's a bungee jump and you can take the leap. You will not hit the ground.

It is only words on paper. It is only the truth you need to tell.

"Writing as I experience it," wrote Jennifer Stone in *Telegraph Avenue Then* in 1992, "means wringing out the heart/mind until it stops lying."

After all, you are not committing to writing because you aim to write witty, insightful descriptions of the neighbor who waters her lawn in her nightgown. Or a description of the man who stands near the vestibule after nine o'clock Mass every Sunday with the Rasputin beard and the Howard Hughes fingernails, his arm linked with that of a birdish, spiky woman wishing you good morning between lips painted messily with dark red lipstick spread far beyond the lines of her mouth.

Mapping It Out

You are writing because your Big Idea is just that: big. So when you rev up the engines and pull away from the curb, you need to have a map of where you're going. Your Big Idea is the map. If you were to just sit behind the wheel and drive off, you may drive in circles or just up and down the driveway, never getting to where you intend to go but emptying the gas tank just the same.

Name the Big Idea in clear, simple language. Make it a declarative statement because you are declaring what you will write about. You may write "I feel trapped in my work" or "I want to be more affectionate to my partner" or "My father hurt me with his anger." But you need to write down the words that will serve as road map of where you want to go and what you want to explore.

Once you name the Big Idea, your journey will be smoother; it will take less time, the route will be more direct, and you won't feel as frustrated. So take out the map and put the pushpin on your Big Idea.

Like fingerprints, your Big Idea is different than anyone else's. It is not too big and it is not too small. It is just right. Commit to following through on your Big Idea. It's the starting point and it is the ignition button. The journey is ahead of you, but with your Big Idea spelled out on paper, you have begun to move ahead.

So write. Writing is like breathing. You need to catch your breath just as you need to catch the ideas, feelings, emotions, and replays of events that are in your head. Catch them before you lose them. Save your breath. Save your life.

Exercises

1. Make a list of the ideas you have in your head and what you want to express in your writing. Beneath each of these ideas, write down what you hope to gain from exploring your feelings and emotions. For instance, if you write down "The trouble with my sister," be specific and write "When we were younger, I felt jealous of her because she was too busy for me." You may also write "clarity" or "calm" or you may want "closure" from an issue you are revisiting about an old friend or a declining marriage. You may also write "holidays" as an idea, but you need to expand on what you mean and explain it specifically: "Holidays are difficult for me because I

feel lonely then." You may choose to write about this specifically because you want to learn why you feel this way.

2. Select one Big Idea from this list to start with today. The Big Idea is a declarative sentence that includes the word *I*. Your Big Idea must be in the active voice, rather than the passive voice. It is much more helpful to write "I ended my relationship because I didn't trust" instead of "My relationship was ended because of a loss of trust." Write your specific feeling or reaction to an event or a relationship. For instance, your Big Idea could be "I am struggling with my diagnosis of cancer," "I am lonely since my son has gone away to college," or "I have never confronted my anger about my father's death." My Big Idea for this book is "I want to share my ideas on writing and how writing helped me save my life."

3. Use your Big Idea as a bumper sticker for your writing. Keep it in front of you as you write so you don't get too far off the point. If you want to explore your feelings of fear in your marriage, don't start writing about the ham and eggs you had for breakfast. Instead, write what is at the heart of your Big Idea. And do your best to stay on course.

This essay ran in the *Chicago Tribune* on June 4, 2000, and prompted more mail than any other story I had written for the paper in more than eleven years. There were letters to the editor empathizing with me, congratulating me for saying people ask such indignant questions constantly. And there were angry letters saying single parents are the downfall of society and I shouldn't damn all fathers; I should be ashamed of myself for not being married.

Big Ideas are larger than the specifics you are writing about. After all, that's why they are Big and they drive your story. On one level, this was an essay about eating out in restaurants alone with my children. But the Big Idea was larger than that. When I wrote it, I was trying to work through my self-consciousness of being a single parent. I wrote about feeling conspicuous and questioned when eating dinner out with my three boys and being treated as incomplete without a husband.

The Big Idea of this essay was not just about an insensitive hostess at a local Thai restaurant; the Big Idea was "I am trying to cope with the stress of being judged as an incomplete family." That is much bigger. That is the Big Idea worth exploring, the bumper sticker for my essay worth sticking on my back window.

Your writing can be about something specific that happened to you, an event, a memory, a part of your history. For anyone who remembers writing English compositions in high school or college, the Big Idea is the theme of your work or the focus sentence. It's the point of what you are trying to accomplish. Writing about this helped me see how others view our family and how I could be more sensitive to other men and women in the same situation.

The Big Idea is not a summary statement. The Big Idea is the whole point of your writing, and it is Big.

A Plea for Singular Sensitivity

"Table for five?"

The new hostess at our favorite Thai restaurant a few miles from home apparently miscounted heads as my three sons and I walked through the door famished, deliriously anticipating our weekly dinner out.

"No, four," I responded, preoccupied with visions of spicy larb kai—that chicken salad with the peanuts, carrots, and lime juice I can never make right at home.

As she veered us to our Formica-topped table, she patted my youngest son, Colin, on his head and asked in a syrup-soaked voice, "Is Daddy parking the car?"

"No," I said more firmly.

"Daddy working late?" she smiled as the boys folded into their seats like mismatched socks out of the dryer, now and forever forgetting to put their napkins on their laps or remove the baseball caps from their heads. By now my eleven-year-old was visibly annoyed and agitated, a state I have only seen about 9 million times in the past two weeks.

"No," I said again. My drill sergeant firmness was completely lost on her, because as she poured us lemon-fresh ice water, she cooed one more time, "Is Daddy joining you later for dinner?"

I contemplated saying yes just to get the satay ordered, wondering whether I should make up some lie involving a dead cell phone, flu, or traffic, but dismissed the hoax since we are regulars and I could not stomach the same scenario again.

Then as only an eleven-year-old could do in his completely disgusted, eye-rolling, animatedly preadolescent venom, Weldon hissed, "That was rude. What's her problem?"

Why does the world assume Daddy is temporarily missing? Why isn't our family accepted as complete? When will we be considered normal and not an oddity deserving curiosity?

Certainly I am no anomaly. The statistics illuminate the reality that there are one heck of a lot of moms having dinner with their kids alone and no, Daddy is not parking the car, Daddy is not coming later, Daddy isn't at home with a toothache. Statistics in 1990 show that more than 7 million women in this country raise children under the age of eighteen alone. Most of us are white—more than 58 percent of us—with 33 percent of African American women raising children without partners.

A growing number of men (more than 1.6 million) are raising their children alone, without the help of Mommy. I imagine for every custodial father who is present day and night for the needs, wants, and dreams of his children, having the universe assume his wife is just taking a nap while he steps up to the plate for a few hours is nothing less than appalling.

Single parents are not all amputees with phantom pain: that

dull, mysterious longing for a parent partner, a limb that is no longer there. We have become whole the way we are. We are not all holding our breaths until we are legitimized into a millennium version of *The Brady Bunch*. Some of us even preferred *Once and Again* before the season finale when the families threatened to combine.

If single parents have the time to fill out the forms—and I finished mine about 1:00 A.M.—the newest United States Census Bureau figures may indeed show an increase from the 1990 figures that reported more than one-fourth of all households in this country as single-parent homes with children. Twenty-five percent of all births in America are to single women. One-fifth of all single-parent homes are run by fathers.

Wake up and read the custody agreement. He is not parking the car. She is not running an errand.

Sure, I expected the question in Disney World. I recently braved a trek to the Land of Mickey Merchandise with odysseys to every ride in each park every day for a week. My first clue as to the difficulty rating of this endeavor should have been when I called the 800 Disney number almost a year earlier and the reservations clerk asked the ages of the children and the adults. When I told her it was just one adult, she paused and asked, "Are you crazy?"

I understand that at two-parent-family-dense destinations such as Disney World, you can expect to confirm the American illusion of a nuclear family (two parents holding the hands of a starry-eyed child) because that's all there is in the commercials. But I have sat through church sermons about the selfishness of parents who create "broken homes." I have read inane advice books on how to parent with the assumption there are two at home working together, and I have fielded thousands of questions from strangers about the absence of a father at each ceremony / party / event / performance / pool / park / museum that it would be a relief if they asked my age, weight, and how much I owe Visa.

The questions make me wonder why at this point we don't get it that every family isn't making room for an accidentally and temporarily absent Daddy. Or Mommy. I expected it years back when the boys were small and I would maneuver a kindergartner, toddler, and infant-in-stroller into the handicapped stall of the ladies room with me because I had no other choice. And trust me, with the three of them in there, I was handicapped.

At first, I didn't mind when well-meaning families would befriend us at swimming pools and innocently ask where Daddy was. When the boys were so young, we looked like someone else should be there. But nearly five years into this, the presumption is lame.

I am sensitive enough not to ask any woman who has visibly gained weight whether she is pregnant. She will be in labor and dilated before I will pretend to even notice she is round. All I'm hoping for—OK, I'm asking—is that when we see a parent alone in the company of children, we don't ask about the other parent. The details are not our business and the answer may even be too painful. With the growing millions of single-parent families, we can all adjust our frame of reference to stop asking the impertinent question.

It's a party of four. Just four.

After enough laughter, fried rice, and cashew chicken had created distance from the initial inquisition and a calm had replaced the storm, I asked the hostess for a carryout container.

"Bringing this home for Daddy?" the woman smiled.

Next time we will have a pizza delivered.

chapter 4

Everyone's a Critic

I have felt at many times that writing has saved my life. It honors my thoughts.

—Beth, Writing to Save Your Life Workshop participant

Truth or Dare

Erin was taller than me and thinner, with freckles across her nose in a sweep of brown and tan. She was my new friend at the pool that summer. It was a hot August afternoon—the kind when you're just getting a little restless and bored with swimming every day and sleeping late, thinking that starting school might not be so bad after all. I must have been going into fourth, maybe fifth grade.

She was standing with her arms crossed over her chest, covering her chlorine-faded tank suit. We all wore tank suits then. We also wore the rubber bathing caps that made your head look smaller than it should, out of proportion like the tops of clothespins. Some of the girls at the pool had the bathing caps with the chin straps that snapped with metal clasps and the fake rubber flowers glued on the top of the crown—daisies mostly—with petals that flapped when you swam and made noises underwater like cloud-muffled thunder on top of your wet, coiled hair.

"No, tell me," I urged her. We were playing a version of that dangerous preadolescent sport Truth or Dare, and she promised to tell me something about me that she had always thought. I was counting on her saying she liked the way I laughed or my haircut with the bangs hanging like a straight-edged valance over my forehead.

She would go first, which was also risky. She could be sweet or she could be ruthless, whatever she chose, but we both knew full well that she was in complete control and that whatever she decided would stain the color of our friendship forever. I was at her mercy.

"Well, I think you're a show-off," she squinted, and then continued in her list of abominable traits she abhorred about me, the way only a ten-year-old girl can do to another girl the same age by the side of the pool in the late August afternoon. "The way you dip your toe in the water to test to see if it's too cold, thinking everybody's looking at you," she said staring through me, with occasional glances toward the marine blue sky. I fought back tears. "And the way you walk to the snack shop in your white cover-up, flipping your hair like you think you're so great," she continued.

She was only beginning. She had more ammunition and was taking aim. Erin took a deep breath and I felt like throwing up. I had that primal, belly-deep urge welling up within me—flight or fight it's called, as I later learned in a college sociology class—but I wanted to scream at her to stop or run to my mother sitting legs crossed in a lounge chair by the side of the pool knitting and chatting, her white-framed sunglasses hiding her eyes. I wanted to beg her to take us all home right now. Right now. Please.

But before she could utter another blow, I mustered up my courage. "I think you're mean and ugly," I said and turned to walk away, my legs feeling like rubber bands flapping on the hot concrete. I felt like hissing or collapsing into tears. The "mean" was justified I thought, for goodness sake; the "ugly" I threw in for vengeance. I had actually planned on telling her I liked her white blonde hair and the way it was three shades lighter at the end of the summer. Of course, I couldn't now.

Uncensored Writing

Erin was uncensored. She did not keep her opinions to herself, as my mother would admonish us to do when my brothers and sisters and I bickered with each other about anything from the way we hit a Wiffle ball to the way we packed our lunches. But then again, I asked for it, so I needed to be braced for what was to come. It still hurt. And I never spoke to her after that, not the rest of that summer or the summers after, still hearing her words spiked with disgust played over and over in my head whenever I saw her dive into the pool.

There are Erins in all of our lives, in all phases of our lives. Judgments of us can be painful to hear and hard to avoid, and we may even ask for the judgments, unaware of what is to follow, the words that paint the air a different, sharper, stronger, deeper color than we imagined. So we are justified in being wary of exposing ourselves, of being vulnerable. Sticks and stones can break your bones, but words can and will hurt you. Words can bruise you, break your heart, and change you. I have always thought that telling someone your unfiltered opinions and being brutally honest is a selfish way to be, a license to be hurtful.

Censoring your comments for the feelings of others is more civilized, compassionate.

But when you are writing to save your life, your feelings must be uncensored, raw, and unfiltered by the fear of reception. No one is judging you. No one else has to read what you have written. You yourself are writing to save your life.

I know you are worried that no matter how you try to safeguard against your work being read, it may happen. Someone you don't want to read it will find it in your desk drawer, open the file, read the journal. Is there someone you trust whom you would allow to read it and who could keep it stored for you? Could you get a safety-deposit box and put it in there? Trust that it cannot be published without your permission. If there is no way to hide what you are writing and you are not ready to tell the truth, perhaps you can write and substitute another name just to feel safer.

The point is not to ruin the life you have with your writing. The point is to save your truth from evaporating and to gain clarity and perspective from writing about your life.

Sometimes I think writing uncensored is like uncurling a roll of film from its canister to develop it. You've seen the machines at the one-hour developing shops, where the clerk places both hands inside the two black sleeves of a minidarkroom, not able to see the film inside, but unwinding it, blindly, and trusting that the film is not exposed. The process of turning this snake of celluloid into photographs of you and your family smiling on a beach or standing in front of the fireplace at Thanksgiving will only work if the film is not exposed to the light. If you expose the film to the light before it is fixed, then all the photos are lost, blackened, ruined. Unsaved.

You need to take your feelings in the canister, unwind them, and write about them, not exposing them to other people to judge them, react to them, or be hurt by them. Chances are high your honest, uncensored emotions could hurt someone else. This is not the goal; this is not your intent. You want to save your life, not hurt the people who dot the landscape of your life like far-off cows spread out across a Wisconsin field, or those who stand firm and unshakable like old Roman cathedrals on the piazza.

Nobody but Yourself

I'm not saying uncensored automatically means cruel, because it doesn't. You may want to write about the love you've never told anyone about, or the secret experience you had that changed you forever. Without the fear of being judged or criticized, you are free to write in detail of what lies beneath the surface, a surface that may have expertly hidden the snakes, monsters, coral, and plankton below.

The fear of being judged for your words or the actions and events contained in your words is a legitimate fear. But your writing need not be for publication and it is not to be judged. This is for you. You need to acknowledge why that fear is there, shake it off because it doesn't apply, and begin to write. "It's the writing, not the being read, that excites me," Virginia Woolf wrote in 1928.

You need to write so you can look at what is inside of you, the way you need to remove a sliver that slides deep into your finger and causes an irritating, dull, throbbing pain. The sliver needs to be removed; you can't wait for it to disappear. You need to force it out with your words, so the skin can heal.

Writing It for Nobody but Yourself

"Who would want to read a book about your life?" he asked, munching a slice of bacon wrapped around a bronze-glazed and glistening water chestnut, the toothpick still poised between his fingers. It was at a holiday cocktail party, the kind with more fussy cookies than table space and a high ratio of six pounds of melted cheese—in chafing dishes of various shapes and sizes—per guest. I didn't know him well; he was the husband of a woman I knew in passing. We had exchanged pleasantries at basketball games and from the stands at baseball games and soccer matches. Occasionally we greeted each other at school recitals. Still, I was stunned.

What do you say to someone who judges you at a cocktail party where you came to relax? I smiled and retreated to the living room, where the side table upheld the trays of vegetable wraps, sliced into thick pucks of cream cheese, cracker bread, lettuce, tomatoes, and cucumbers. I prayed he would stay away from me. I hadn't come here to be judged or grow defensive.

None of us are prepared to be judged. I left early, picked up my coat, put it on in the hallway where the mahogany table was stocked with polite hostess gifts, went home, paid the baby-sitter, and breathed deeply.

Who would want to read about your life?

You would, because you need to honor your story with words that validate your experiences. You need to give your story some air, some sunlight, some breathing room. You need to bring your story out into the open with words on paper, and invite no one else to take them in. This one's for you.

You want to read them because you know they are there. Putting them into words makes them real again, gives them life and substance.

Placing your words on paper is like bringing a drooping houseplant to the windowsill where the sun is so bright it fills every corner of the room. Here is the sunlight; now your plant can thrive. You did no more than move the plant to a new place; you did no more than move the words you hear in your head and in your heart onto the paper. Writing down your experiences moves them to a new place in the sun where they can grow and your understanding of your history can flower.

Moving Past the Censorship

"Writing has been a way of explaining to myself the things I do not understand," poet Rosario Castellanos wrote more than thirty years ago.

When you shift your understanding of writing to be something personal and you-centered, rather than being something available for someone else to judge and to criticize, then the immobilizing fear of being judged will fall away. You will outgrow the use of it, no longer feeding it; it will wither and move on. Like a family of possums who have adopted an open garbage can for a nightly meal, once the source is gone, the animals will move somewhere else.

Don't feed the fear.

But maybe the critic you fear most is not some jerk at a cocktail party or some little girl by the side of the pool. Maybe the critic you fear most is you. I understand that. But editing yourself before you give yourself a chance will not release the story inside of you. Censoring yourself will keep your story inside where it is dark and secret. Give yourself a chance. Take a chance on yourself.

When I started to write this book, I was puffed up with all I wanted to share and all I knew to be true. A few chapters into it, I allowed my fear of being an imposter to multiply and sit near my computer keyboard as a big, bad-breath invisible monster staring at me as I typed every sentence. Writer Anne Lamott talks about the voices of critics in your head plaguing you as you write. Author Julia Cameron writes about the need to let go of these voices in order to fulfill your creativity.

Some people need to embody and personify the critic into a schoolteacher with a red pen and a sour look to be able to move past the fear of judgment. That may help because we have all graduated beyond that teacher, even if we have not forgotten her. We need not assign her any more power. She is not grading your writing anymore.

Getting Over Yourself

In order to find the courage to keep writing, I tell myself what I tell my children whenever they are consumed and overcome by minutiae and spend exorbitant amounts of vocal energy on losing one baseball card or not having their favorite T-shirt out of the dryer yet. I calmly say, "Get over yourself." It is such a great phrase. I am contemplating painting it in gold script high on the kitchen wall where they are sure to see it every morning as they fight over who gets what flavor bagel or who looked at whom during breakfast.

I also show my workshop students and graduate students a simple exercise. I take a column of mine that was in the newspaper (I'm not brave enough yet to take a copy of my first book and do this), and I throw it on the floor. I then proceed to stomp on it, yell expletives at it, and tell it that it stinks. Then I tear it in pieces and throw it in the garbage.

"I am still here," I tell my students and smile. Whatever criticism erupts from writing my words, it does not change who I am. I will not starve or suddenly lose my friends and family because I dared to write down my story. Nor will you. I also use the exercise to show students concretely that I am my own worst critic. As far as I know, no one else is stomping, hissing, spitting, and swearing at anything I have written. Like I said, as far as I know.

Write what you need to write. No one else will judge it. And don't you judge yourself for your writing. Erin was just a little girl by the side of a swimming pool who saw the opportunity to feel powerful and seized it. The man at the cocktail party perhaps had a dozen manuscripts of his own in a basement drawer. I can't let the writing be about either of them. Nor can you make it about anyone in your life who embodies criticism. And I can't let the writing stop because I am afraid when I am compared to all the great writers I admire, I will come up miserably short. I can't be in my own way, and I can't let the writing stop because of my own self-effacing insecurities.

Being Honest

Write for yourself. Even if in the back of your mind you are hoping to self-publish your book, or be discovered, or be the next Dave Eggers with a best-selling first memoir, don't write for an audience. Don't confuse your writing with the need for approval. Write for honesty's sake. Write for writing's sake.

Write for the you who is free from the fear of judgment. Write for the you who comes in the door from work and wears the slouchiest sweatpants because they are soft and comfortable and you've worn them since college. Write for the you who wakes up in the morning refreshed before remembering anything that needs to be done for anyone.

Write for the you who puts french fries between the buns of the cheeseburger in spite of jeers from friends. Write for the you who listens to Barry White tapes and dances for hours. Write for the you who has cold lasagna for breakfast—straight out of the refrigerator, eating it with your hands. Write for the you who sometimes doesn't want to dwell on what other people think. Write for the you who is still innocent, before having an inkling about Erins at swimming pools and men at cocktail parties who say things that deflate you as quickly as if you were a party balloon and they had stabbed you with a toothpick. Don't censor yourself because limiting your words and stifling your truth will not help you heal.

"An honest tale speeds best being plainly told," William Shakespeare wrote in *Richard III*.

Write freely. Write to be free of the fear of what will happen when you write the truth.

But write.

Exercises

1. Write down the names of all the people you fear may criticize you or judge you for telling the truth. This list could include people in your family, friends, or people you are writing about. Next to their names, write the words *I will never let them read this*. Make this promise to yourself and do what you need to do to ensure your privacy and keep the sanctity of your words honored.

2. When you are done with exercise 1, write in big letters *I will write anyway.* Fold this up and place it in your wallet, put it in your makeup bag or your gym workout bag, tape it to your computer, or put it in your sock drawer where you will see it every day. This is an affirmation that underlines your journey. No matter what you can concoct as an excuse not to write, you have the answer: "I will write anyway." Good luck.

3. Make a list of how you feel when you write without fear of judgments. Is it the feeling you get when you're swimming alone? Is it the feeling you get when you are driving on an open road? Is it the same as when you dance alone or sing in the shower? Close your eyes and imagine yourself doing one thing that makes you feel free and unjudged. Now tell yourself this is how you can feel when you write without fear of being judged.

We are surrounded by judgments. We are judged by the way we look, act, work, live. Our children are judged by a thousand different yardsticks. We are judged by how our children are judged.

In early 2000 I was struggling with the pressure of my children being judged and compared and how the lives they led could not be simple. Having my three boys all in school for the first time and being involved daily with other parents, I found quickly that teachers, parents, and classmates are eager to categorize and label. I was having a hard time, mostly because I adore my children and hate to see them disappointed in a culture where being the best is all they are taught to value.

I was quickly growing tired of the judgments they faced constantly. I wrote then about how I was even afraid to stand up to those judgments in my writing. The following essay helped me see more clearly the way I felt and why it bothered me: not that my sons would never excel, but that they were always being measured. Writing is that way. If you write to be judged, then your writing will suffer, and it will take you longer to get to the truth because you will be writing for someone else.

This story originally ran in the *Chicago Tribune* and Colin's kindergarten teacher hung it outside her classroom in the hallway. It was quoted in a friend's PTO newsletter. I was frustrated that my children felt pressured to excel in everything they did before school, in school, during sports, and after school. It was no longer just OK to have fun and try hard. It became important for them to be the best in everything. I paraphrased for them what I heard Julia Cameron say in one of her workshop tapes: It's not crowded at the top. It's crowded at the bottom.

Not everyone can win first place; not everyone has to. The process of writing has to be the goal, without fear of judgment and the wish for a gold medal. We can't write when we are stricken with the cold fear that we will be picked last for volleyball. We can't write honestly and uncensored when we are preoccupied with the reception of the outcome. But we can write when we let the judgment of ourselves go. We can then accept what is there and what we write.

Average Is OK with Her

I thought about saying this wasn't really about me. I thought about saying it was really my friend who has three boys, ages eleven, nine, and six, or someone I know from car pool, met once, recognized from church, read a story about, or is a cousin of a good friend who lives somewhere remote, maybe Wyoming. You don't regularly bump into people from Wyoming who could expose your truth.

But the world does not need one more parent who stretches the truth like a party clown fashioning a balloon into a dachshund, elephant, or hat, however well intentioned. What I feel conditioned to apologize for is something that should be accepted readily. What makes me defensive is that in a lot of ways, when measured by the world's yardstick, my three children are average.

Average: It's a parent's dirty word.

It seems that most everyone I know has children who are genuinely exceptional, stunning. They ride horses and win ribbons; they enter science fairs and win scholarships; they sing for the governor, the president, an occasional monarch. They are the best in their age group at soccer, basketball, swimming, tennis, football, baseball, gymnastics, and academics. And I'm happy for them, really, as I imagine these wizard progeny profoundly cooperative and cheerfully greeting each new, triumphant day with awards granted, prizes won—accumulating more trophies, badges, medals, and plaques for the family mantel.

Then I realize the stress my children are under to excel, to be superior, to make it to the top in anything and everything they try in school and after school. Average doesn't cut it anymore. You have to come in first. Not only do you have to make the honor roll, but be at the top of the honor roll. You have to be picked for the solos in the music programs, kick the winning goal, dunk the winning basket. If not, you're nothing. You're not even a contender.

There has been a lot written lately about the average grades achieved by a school-age Albert Einstein. But his record is dismissed with a relieved sigh because he did end up on the cover of *Time* at the end of the century. That was the point, right?

It's not that I'm jealous or allergic to competition. It's just that excelling for children seems mandatory and exponentially more exaggerated than when I was growing up. I tried to do well in school not because my parents planned to post my grades on the billboard off the Eisenhower Expressway but because I liked school and loved to read.

When I was growing up, there was inherent competition in our house anyway, with six of us born in less than eight years. My parents were not the sort who screamed at us during swim meets, like some of the fathers I still remember, fists clenched, faces contorted in fury, neck muscles bulging if their child's time was slow. All of us were on the country-club swim team, and I showed the least promise of all. The two-foot, second-place golden statue I have with the faux marble base was won by default. There were three of us in the four- to six-year-old age group in 1963, and the best swimmer was out with pneumonia for most of the season.

But even if I never had won a trophy, I knew in every cell and in every twist on my DNA that my parents adored me.

I hope I communicate that to my children, but it seems harder these days, what with all their friends invited to the White House, breaking state records, launching new companies, and all. I want my boys to know that whoever they are and whatever they do, it is fine as long as they do their best and not give up—that my love is unconditional.

I want them to know I think they are the most special, brilliant, original, creative, amusing, and illuminating children on the face of the planet. I want them to fully understand that while it's a lot of fun to stand in front of a school assembly and have everyone applaud, it can't be everything. And it can't be everything for me.

I know it's countertrend, but instead of posting their daily achievements on a family Web site, I try to honor the stolen moments privately, such as the image of my oldest son, Weldon, being an altar server at his first Sunday Mass. His face was pristine and innocent as he sat on the velvet bench, his feet swinging wildly, untamable below his robes, his legs too short to reach the ground. I cherish Brendan, who argues it is the "Golf" of Mexico because you can play the sport there, and who recently told me all he needs from me are fifteen seconds of hugs each day. And then there's my youngest, Colin, who is mercurial, mischievous, and sweet, and who proclaimed one morning, "I have a big life!"

Truthfully, I am glad for the parents who have children who win the top honors. But it can't be what drives me as a mother; I can't take their scorecards personally. While it would be gratifying to see their pictures on the cover of the local paper, it has to be enough to see them grow gracefully from the raucous, kinetic boys they are now into good men, good husbands, and good fathers who are genuine, caring, and joyful, who leave behind scrapbooks not filled with first-place ribbons but with photographs of smiles.

And if that is average, I'll take it.

chapter 5

Quiet Down

Shhhh . . . Mommy's writing.

—Hand-painted sign on the knob of my bedroom door

Listening to Your Heart

I have found that the best way to write is to be quiet and listen to your own stirrings, undistracted. How else can you hear what your heart is saying?

When I was a teenager living in the house on Jackson Avenue and Augusta Boulevard, my sisters and I shared a Montgomery Ward record player. I stacked the speakers on top of the highboy dresser that is now in my son Weldon's room, where he places his soccer, baseball, and basketball trophies.

When I was his age, the turntable was up there, perched above the drawers, so you needed to stand on a chair or footstool to place an album on the spindle and flick on the black plastic switch, making sure it was set to thirty-three. You could also play 45s on the turntable if you snapped the colored plastic disk in the center of the record.

I would listen to Led Zeppelin, Grand Funk Railroad, Deep Purple, the Rolling Stones, and Foghat, plus anything else loudly repetitious with un-recognizable lyrics that all the other teens at Oak Park–River Forest High

School listened to at the highest volume possible. All this of course was when my mother wasn't home.

The furniture shook and offered a twanging bass to the thunder generating from the dresser top. I would play my favorite songs over and over and over, picking up the needle by hand, placing it back down on just the right beginning groove until the same, familiar scratching, droning, and screeching started all over again. There were so many bumps and skips and so much dust on each record that the background for every song sounded like a Rambler station wagon pulling in a gravel driveway over and over and over again, up and back, up and back.

The Louder the Better

I loved loud music. Everyone I knew loved loud music. If it wasn't loud, it wasn't good. I remember going to a freshman dance in a high school gym—they were always in a gym—with a ramshackle band on stage who definitely didn't look old enough to drive. For about thirty minutes they played the background chords and chorus from the Rolling Stones's "Sympathy for the Devil."

The lead singer kept imploring in his best mock-British scream, "Whooh, whooh. Whooh, whooh. Whooh, whooh." No other lyrics, just "Whooh, whooh." My friend Barb and I loved it, though later we wondered why they never sang anything else. Maybe they couldn't remember the words.

You need to remember the words.

As teens, we played music loud on the car radio. We danced near the speakers at proms, dressed in long, tight dresses, our hair set exaggeratedly high and round for the event. I would go to parties and come home hoarse from trying to shout over the music.

Fortunately I turned the corner on loud when I was about twenty, after my second Bruce Springsteen concert when I was a junior at Northwestern University, sitting in the fourth row feeling as if the scream-singing of my idol was coming from my chest cavity. I couldn't hear myself clear my throat. My head pounded and my ears hurt. Everyone else in the arena was screaming as loud as they could and they all appeared to love every ear-pounding moment. I may well have been the only one there that night who thought it was too loud. Bruce looked like he loved it too.

I guess when I was very young I didn't want to hear what my heart had to say. Or maybe it didn't have all that much to say. I'm older now and much different. I need the quiet to think and write. I have transformed into one of those adolescent-dreaded adults who is always asking—no, requiring—their children and the friends of their children to "turn it down, please."

Quiet, please. Please be quiet.

The White Noise of Life

I don't understand writers who claim they need to listen to a certain type of music in order to write. Some insist on classical music, with a favorite movement to write fiction by, or a jazz CD they choose when they are blocked from inspiration. Some say they favor sultry chanteuses or brooding Latin romantics.

In order to write, I want only the white noise of life. I like the hum of the cars passing by, the occasional wind gust that flaps the awnings outside the window, or the caw of an arrogant crow who sits on the front lawn recovering from a bout with the squirrels. I like the swish of the dishwasher, the baritone of the refrigerator, the occasional plunk, plunk, plunk of the ice maker. The whoosh of the heat coming on in the winter and the drone of the air conditioner in summer. I turn off the ringer and let voice mail answer the phone.

This is as much noise as I want to hear, because if the noise is more intricate, I pay attention to that instead of the silence. If I listen to music, I will pay attention to the melody, the words, or the rhythm outside of me instead of inside of me.

Sarah Orne Jewett wrote in a 1908 letter to Willa Cather, "You must find your own quiet center of life and write from that to the world." The words hold true almost a century later.

I agree. Perhaps I relish the quiet because most of the time my life is not quiet. I need to manufacture calm; quiet does not appear in my life unless scheduled and forced. A friend of mine said that when she calls my house, the cacophony that erupts occasionally on my end makes it sound as if she is calling a prison during an uprising. My boys shout to each other from room to room, floor to floor, and even attempt to communicate to each other from the yard to the family room. I feel sorry for the neighbors on the days when the doors and windows are open—especially if all the boys have friends over to play.

I haven't always needed quiet to write. Working in Dallas on a daily newspaper, I thrived on the frenzy of the features department and the buzz of the newsroom. It was so *Lou Grant*, so *Mary Tyler Moore Show*. It was like a set of a 1940s newspaper movie, an act from *Front Page* in which reporters and editors are yelling across desks and screaming into phones, jumping up and down from their chairs as the stories seem to spontaneously combust on the page, the staff needed to extinguish the flames.

So much energy, it was almost palpable. The pressroom was in the belly of the *Dallas Times Herald* building, and as you sat in the features department on the third floor at your computer with thirty other writers also at their computers or on the phones, you could hear the groans and clicks of the presses beneath your feet.

The Quiet Within

But I was doing a different kind of writing then, mostly reporting and retelling stories of what happened moments, hours, or days earlier. It was somewhat formulaic, a public journalism of information and exposition of stories that needed to be told from people who needed to tell them.

I tried to creatively use all of myself, but even when I stretched to invent smooth sentences that had a certain melody, I had not accessed my heart in my work. Not really. My writing then was about superficial judgments and quick descriptions, paragraphs built on phrases I crafted to recreate a scene on deadline.

I hadn't done any of the writing from a place that was deeper, more private, and mine-filled and without a neat beginning, middle, and end, the kind of writing I was not taught in journalism school. For me, that deep kind of writing requires quiet because the thoughts can slip away from you like fireflies, flashing their brilliance once before they are gone.

I need to concentrate and pull at the words, using the quiet as a backdrop to summon my own wisdom. It's as if you are fishing for the words to tell what you need to say. You are quiet in the still of predawn, in your boat or on a gray wooden pier. You sit quietly. You let the words come to the surface. Call them out with your bait and your willingness to hear them. Write them down.

I don't mean to say that words come of their own volition. It is you who needs to retrieve them. Unlike some writers who insist their stories emerge of their own accord, while the writers somehow serve as mediums in a trance, I have found that the writing you need to do to free yourself and heal yourself is all about your effort of extricating it from within. It is an intellectually and emotionally active and athletic process.

You need to call to your words, beckon them, listen for them, and offer them a safe place to arrive. If there is too much confusion and noise, the words inside you will retreat, like fish who see your wiggling feet and the splashing water and sense the bait is a trap.

Writing is not passive, and it doesn't happen without you, to you, or in spite of you. When I have done writing that is raw and honest, I am exhausted and energized at the same time, the way you feel after running or walking a mile very fast. But it takes energy and concentration and a commitment to the Big Idea.

Inviting the Words In

You cannot just open the window and expect your life story to flutter in accidentally and land on you. You need to open the window in a place that is quiet, call to the words and the story inside of you, and ask yourself what it is you need to say. If there is too much noise, you will not have the presence of mind to know the right questions to ask. The window will be closed.

I know some people can write in cafés and in train stations, in diners and in busy parks alive with children, dogs, and rapid, loud soccer games. They get to a zone, and as some say, they write in flow. I think it needs to be a quiet zone. If the noise is not there, you don't need to block it out and you have already begun with an advantage. There is nothing you need to erase. I suggest you eliminate the step of blocking out the noise and begin with a quiet place. A quiet zone.

Quiet isn't just about the absence of noise. It is about the presence of peace and calm. It is about the absence of distraction and thoughts that call you away from where you need to be and what you need to write. Some of these distractions are your excuses and your fears, but some are simply details and practical considerations of what you need to do to get through life.

You need to think about how to get from here to there, how to transport a child or a parent or a friend from place to place, how to get your work done, when to clean your house, when to shop for groceries, what to get when you get there, when to pick up the draperies at the cleaners. I understand all of this. You can't ignore it all, but you can suspend some of the urgency for a little piece at a time.

You need to create for yourself a quiet zone of white noise, without the noise of your own distractions, the must-do's and the have-to's. But I am not suggesting you can ignore it all. The rest of the universe will not fall away and comply with your needs.

You do have to feed your family. You have to go to work. You need to go to school. You have to sleep. You have to fix dinner. You have to shower, walk the dog, return the phone calls, and help your children with homework. You have to take out the garbage, and you have to visit your mother. But not at midnight. Or at 6:00 A.M. At midnight or 6:00 you can find the quiet place you need to write. There is some quiet zone in your life, however minimal or forced, and you need to access it. Whether you wake up twenty minutes earlier or go to sleep twenty minutes later, you can find the time to manipulate your schedule for writing.

We are not all able to be the chosen writers at Yaddo, a safe writer's haven where meals are served three times a day in a bucolic, historic, celebrity setting. Where residents write poetically and freely, the next Pulitzer Prize–winning novel, the next critically acclaimed play. We can't all walk away from what we do in the rest of our lives to write about our lives. But we can all carve a sanctuary of quiet in the lives we are already living.

The Color of Quiet

It is unrealistic to suggest that in order to write to save your life you have to stop living your life and suspend all the obligations you have at work, in your family, and with your friends. As a single parent, I know that 90 percent of my life is immutable and spoken for with work and family. Regardless of anything I need or want to do, the needs of my children come first. I am their parent and they rely on me for food, clothing, shelter, and just about everything else.

But 10 percent of my life I get to play with. That 10 percent needs to be quiet so I can write. And I make sure I make it quiet.

If quiet were a color, I think it would be a translucent yellowish gold, all warm and honey-smooth. It is the color of my living room where I love to lie and read, where the boys love to sit on the couch and talk, where Brendan wants to retreat under a brown velour blanket when he is tired and over-whelmed. It is the color of sunlight.

I took a painting class in high school from an art teacher named Sandy who painted enormous, photo-realistic figures of women as winged angels. She walked with a kind of earned freedom, confident and comfortable with her body, her long, brightly colored linen dresses and skirts almost liquid the way they hung about her and swayed when she moved across the room from student to student at each easel, commenting on each work in progress.

She wore enormous, chunky bracelets: colored wooden beads the size of throat lozenges, stacked one on the other like horseshoes in a game of back-yard toss, covering a third of her forearm. She also wore impossibly large ear-rings and necklaces made of chunky, bagel chip–size beads at her throat, so she made wind-chime music wherever she went.

I thought her compelling in a forbidden, bohemian kind of way, so unlike the other, more predictably stiff teachers who taught the requisite courses of biology, geometry, and history. If they were like Saltine crackers, then she was like chocolate mousse. She seemed like the kind of teacher I could tell any-thing to and she would keep the secret. She seemed so daring, so alive, and she permitted us all to feel the same. I loved her weekly class, and because of how I felt in those forty minutes, I loved Tuesdays.

She taught us to invent the illusion of light on our canvases by washing them with very thin layers of watered-down cadmium yellow. Just a touch of yellow in each plastic container of water would drench the canvas in the thinnest coat of pale, pale light when painted sparingly in wide, even strokes. The theory was when you painted on top of it, the light came through from beneath.

Writing is like that. Let the quiet be your canvas so the words can come from within, in layers upon layers, filling your scene with light and meaning that come from beneath. The words are the light and you can layer upon the quiet of a blank, white canvas your thoughts and memories, your details, emotions, and insights.

You cannot paint the image in your mind with ease onto a canvas that is already covered, filled from edge to edge and bustling with other colors and images. You can't paint your picture unless the canvas is bare. You cannot write in a place that is already filled with the noise of other things, other distractions, other duties, and other people.

Prepare a blank canvas. Prepare a quiet zone. Fill the space with your silence, so when you call to the words, you can hear them answer you. Write them down.

Exercises

1. Plan when and how you can achieve quiet. Will it be when everyone else in the house has gone to bed? Will it be before work, about 6:00 A.M.? Will it be on your lunch hour when you can take a walk or retreat to a library? Look at your calendar and see what days appear more free for you. Plan those days as writing days, when you will come home from work or school and write before dinner or before bed. Don't reschedule or you will keep procrastinating.

2. Turn off the TV. Unplug the phone. Turn off the radio and the CD player. Ask everyone in your life to respect your need for a chunk of silence. Give yourself a quiet zone. For fifteen minutes, a half hour, maybe two hours, let yourself be quiet and sit with your thoughts. You have your Big Idea; now you can begin to write in response to it. Just write. Write what comes into your head and don't worry whether it makes sense. Just write. Whether you write longhand in a journal or on a pad of lined paper, or type your words on a computer or typewriter, the point is the writing. Any method will help you reach your goal of writing your story.

3. Make an agreement with yourself to create a quiet zone regularly. Schedule it on your wall calendar or in your daybook. Write it on your to-do list. You need to do this for yourself. Find the quiet place and pull out the words. Write what you mean to say. Follow this as religiously as you honor all your other obligations. After all, you find the time for haircuts regularly. You find the time for the gym. You eat three times a day. Now find the time for writing regularly. Commit to the writing and to the quiet. Listen to what is inside you and acknowledge what you need to say. Write it down.

This essay originally ran in the *Chicago Tribune* on October 13, 1997. I had been trying to keep it all together for almost two years as a single parent. What I found was that I desperately needed quiet and time alone to be able to juggle everything life was passing my way. Writing this helped me to see that it isn't so silly to cherish the moments spent alone in the bathtub, that it is equal to a trip to a spa. My time in the bathtub is a quiet zone.

A Bath Just Has to Be Enough

I take baths. A few nights week when my three children are in bed and no one is coughing, crying, or shouting jokes to the ceiling, I wash my hair and read foolish magazines that have no larger social message, nothing but beautiful people in absurd clothes looking hungrily at the camera. I lie there in my stolen serenity, flipping pages until I get good and red in a tub too hot for children, in a tub all by myself.

"Four minutes, Mom. Your shower was four minutes," my nine-year-old told me after clocking my usual rushed ritual on his new stopwatch, a birthday gift from his Aunt Maureen. "You were in there a long time," he noted. Four minutes is usually all the time I have. The untimed bath is a special luxury.

"What do you do for yourself?" my friends—as well as strangers—ask me. It seems to be the topic of many of those magazines I read in the tub, on the evenings the laundry is already emptied from those bright green baskets filled with mismatched socks and Batman underpants, blue jeans thin at the knees, and T-shirts with sayings cryptic and brightly painted.

The answer is I take a bath.

I have friends who vacation with other friends. I know women who take classes or play tennis. Many shop—lots of them shop. My sister Madeleine swears by the magic touch of a masseuse whose facial massage can erase the bad memories of the last two to five years. I ponder the mailed brochures for the classes on spirituality, pottery, figure drawing, or Thai cooking and toss them away. I agree it would be euphoric to take all of these every week, in order to expand, to grow, to reach beyond my life. But for now all I can do is take a bath.

While not an advocate for martyrdom, I tell my friends who espouse the evening classes and the long weekends away that the only thing that makes sense to me is to stay home, put my children to bed happy, rest, and heal. I'm not saying answering the same question fifteen times from those little faces close to the ground does not make me raw. I'm not saying the whirling needs and noise of three boys is not at times fodder for insanity. But right now a bath has to be enough.

Some nights when I soak in my white tub surfing through humid catalogs of impossibly luxurious clothes, table lamps, and sofas, I look back on the day and am amazed that all that has passed is twenty-four hours. Working hard, caring for three alone, and recovering from what is best described as a dropkick to my heart has taken the adventurer out of me. It has taken away the woman who stays up late sewing fringe on pillows, or finishing watercolor still lifes for the dining room.

What has been born in her place is a woman who finds solace in a bath with an alternating fragrance menu of vanilla, apricot, honey, or gardenia. "Doing for myself" means enjoying the silence of knowing I am safe at home with three sons who dream well.

I remember the longing I had for them before they were born, before I forever knew their smiles, dimples, and freckles, the way their eyes droop when they don't feel well, the way their eyes shine when they do. And I distinctly remember that the motivation for having my children was I did not want my epitaph to read "She did so many wonderful things for herself."

Five Minutes' Peace is a book a woman gave me after we met at a seminar two years ago. It is a children's book about a mother elephant who wants to take a bath without her three little elephants bothering her. I love the book and read it often to the boys, who laugh at the pictures. I remember the daylong seminar and how it rejuvenated me. But two years have passed since and I haven't had time to take another.

I would love to swim every day, have a massage, and learn to sew, really sew like my grandmother did. I would love to paint again, to feel that joy of brush to paper or canvas and savor the lightness of creativity. I would like to exercise every night and wake up one morning looking like Ashley Judd. And I would love to read a new book every day, not just a few pages of the same one I can't seem to finish.

But as a mother I know that doing any of these things for myself is not high on the list or even in the cards. Nor can it be. As a single mother in a peculiar and fragile situation, the constraints of sunrise and sunset make it nearly impossible for me to steal more than a few moments alone.

To do so would mandate my absence from a dinner of macaroni and cheese with three blue-eyed boys babbling about bikes or bullies or both. It would mean not helping Brendan to read. It would mean no snuggles with Colin. I find the reliable rhythm of steadily forming their lives a grounding melody. It is a beautiful, soulful tedium and right now that's all I want to do. Followed, of course, by a very long bath.

chapter 6

Open the Door

I thought I had passed through various feelings, but writing this forced
me to feel everything again. I've never written from this place before
and it's scary and painful, and in a strange way, illuminating.

—Valerie, Writing to Save Your Life Workshop participant

Entering All the Rooms

At my brother Paul's house, a local mural artist celebrated for his commissioned works painted a garden scene on the walls of the foyer. The mural is two stories high. From the front door to the walls wrapping around the staircase are intricately detailed stone walls, ivy, hydrangeas, and bougainvillea so realistic you could almost sneeze. Butterflies dot the blue-washed sky. A bench beckons you for a rest. You feel a serenity and cheerfulness you just don't get from your average off-white entranceway.

You open the door and are transported.

Writing is like that. When you begin to write, you are opening the door to what lies inside of you. You can be opening the door to a large house, with many rooms you haven't dared to enter in years, and other rooms you have forgotten exist. Some rooms feel intimidating and frightening; some rooms are menacing with the throbbing memories they contain. But some rooms are so familiar and comfortable, it is as if the carpet is worn beneath your feet as you walk through, peering into each doorway. You know the sights and smells of the house and it feels safe.

Don't be afraid of opening the door. Don't tell yourself the door is blocked and place imaginary furniture in front of the door saying you cannot get to the writing. Imagine it is an unlocked door with free and easy access.

Varying Degrees of Memory

As you start writing, it could feel like entering a dark house at first, but your writing will turn on the lights as you walk from room to room: now the kitchen, next the dining room, the laundry room, the family room, the living room, the den, the bedrooms. The memories you will uncover in your writing will be distinctly different in texture and translucence. Some memories will be bright and glaring, like the white light over the kitchen sink. Other recollections will be hazier and dreamlike, like the dim glow from a Tiffany lamp in a guest room with sheer curtains and a slight September breeze.

In 1892 Charlotte Perkins Gilman wrote the short story "The Yellow Wallpaper," in which her character's obsession with the design and figures in the pattern of the wallpaper and the details of the one room where she stays with her husband become the springboard for her leap into madness. "I don't know why I should write this. I don't want to. I don't feel able. I know John would think it absurd. But I must say and do what I think in some way—it is such a relief."

I'm not saying that opening the door will send you lurching into insanity. I'm saying that when you open the door and write what is there, the writing becomes about much more than just the details. The writing is about you.

You may be afraid to write because of what you might find when you open the door. You could be afraid that you will open the door and see a blank, brick wall. It could be a false door, like pockets that are sewn shut on a suitcoat or merely just flaps of material for show. You may also fear that once you open the door you'll career down the elevator shaft like a toon in *Who Framed Roger Rabbit?*

But I promise you there is something beyond the door, because you have a past and you have experiences. Your life is not blank. You will not face a blank wall if you are patient and willing to quiet down and accept the process of writing. You will not slam head-on into something immovable like Evel Knievel or his son missing the mark on a motorcycle jump. You will not open the door and slam into the side of the Grand Canyon.

You will not free-fall down an elevator shaft because you can stop the writing when you feel too much. You can get help; you can seek support. The writing is voluntary; the writing is free. No one can push you. You don't have to jump, and you don't have to fall two stories. You can open the door and peer inside at your own pace. You can build your safety net with your own words.

The discovery begins when you open the door and allow yourself to walk into the rooms of your history and write down what you see. You can walk into the rooms in the order that feels most comfortable. Write down what it felt like, what it looked like, how you feel now. Writing about your life does not have to be a recreation of *The Haunting*, with ghosts and monsters looming larger and more treacherous with every passing minute.

Writing can be the same as cautiously taking the sheets off the furniture you are preserving from dust and rummaging through the past to find the treasures and the meaning that you left behind. Writing can make you feel better as you clear out the trunks you have been carting inside of you that weigh you down, that make you heavy.

I tell my students at Northwestern they will be better writers by paying attention to the details everywhere they go: in the elevator, on the street, in the cafeteria, on the train or the bus, in each room they enter, even in the classroom. Sometimes after a half hour or so of me lecturing, I tell them to describe what I am wearing in a few paragraphs and then I walk quickly out of the room. They all panic, but about a third of them can remember the colors, the details. Some even recall the earrings I was wearing and how I wore my hair. A whole lot of them get it wrong. Strive to get it right.

Exploring Childhood Adventures

The details of your memories are what will make the writing more meaningful. What do you remember about the rooms of your heart? What truth can you no longer hide? What room do you need to enter again and again to understand?

When I was a young girl, there was a somewhat obnoxious board game I loved, Mystery Date, that I played with my sisters and with my friends when they came to visit. I even remember the commercial for the popular game with a chorus of girlish voices singing, "Open the door to your . . . mystery date. Will it be a dream boat?" (This part of the song is punctuated by sighs and sounds of general amorous wooziness.) "Or a dud?" The dud choice was the one that was aimed at repulsing us completely, with his disheveled clothes and his greasy hair. This was the kind of young man my father would not let into the house. I rather liked his smile but would never admit it.

I hope a new generation of preteens is not spending afternoons playing a game where their happiness depends on who stands beyond the door on a blind date. But the point of the game was that opening the door was key to earning points and winning the game. Just like writing. It's not so far-fetched a comparison, because when you let down your guard, ignore the fear and criticism of writing, you open the door to possibilities. You find the answer. You win the game.

Taking a Risk

There was a game show I loved on TV that I would watch in the afternoons following morning kindergarten. After a lunch of a boiled hot dog wrapped in a single slice of white bread, daintily dipped bite by bite into a pond of ketchup, I slipped into the white-paneled family room (really a former porch where my parents had added windows and heat). Then I turned on *Let's Make a Deal* as my mother cleared the dishes and turned on the dishwasher.

You may remember the show with Monty Hall, the wryly cheerful host who each day implored guests to rummage through their purses and pockets hunting for corkscrews, dictionaries, plaid underpants, and baited fishhooks, all for a chance to choose a curtain and win what was behind it.

It seemed a dizzying choice, but not as heartbreaking as Sophie's choice in William Styron's novel, where a mother must choose which child will be spared and which child will die at the hands of the Nazis. It seemed more like the blooming, life-changing opening of the door in the movie *An Affair to Remember*, when Cary Grant suddenly gets it that the reason Deborah Kerr can't get off the couch isn't because she's tired or rude but because she is paralyzed. He whisks open her bedroom door and sees the portrait he painted of her on her wall, the same portrait his agent sold to a woman in a wheelchair.

In the seconds after opening the door, he puts all the puzzle pieces together and realizes the agony of being apart was not because she found someone else to love or somehow lost interest in him (didn't he get it that he was Cary Grant after all?), but because she was afraid to let him know she couldn't walk and didn't want to be a burden to him. I bought the movie at a sale bin at Walgreen's for $6.99 one holiday, and I've probably seen the movie thirty times since. I still cry every time he rushes to embrace her after he opens that one door and realizes everything.

Will the door you open in your writing sadden you, surprise you, or validate you? Will it change your outlook and make you see everything clearly? How do you pick? Will it be like *Let's Make a Deal*, and you get something ridiculous like a goat, something luxurious like a cruise for two to the Bahamas, or better yet, your own boat?

I loved the show because to me at age five, the game was about possibilities and taking risks. Risk was something that lured me, even if risk at that age was wearing braids instead of ponytails, or crossing the street alone.

Making the Selection

I agree it is a risk to open the door in your writing. But once you have decided to do it, how do you pick which door to enter first? Do you pick curtain number 1, number 2, or number 3? How do you decide which curtain to open? The answer is that, unlike the game show, there is no wrong answer. Whatever you find in your writing will be worthwhile. It will be a memory you honor; a piece of your life and your past that you chronicle. You simply open the door to the house by allowing yourself to feel and to write what it is you need to write.

I know this sounds like something mysterious you would hear in a *Star Wars* prequel. You may think I am full of myself and that I am acting as if I am so wise and know what is behind every door, like the producers of the game show who had to arrange for the speedboat, the full-length fur, or the eight-foot snake.

The truth is I can't tell you what is behind your doors or even what your door may look like to you. But I can tell you that the doors I have opened in my writing needed to be opened when I opened them. Whether I was writing about my childhood, my marriage, my children, my friendships, or my work, I began to see what was there and the feelings I harbored. And though some rooms were very painful to look into, some made me cry and some made me exhausted, I was always glad—eventually—that I did.

You need to write your Big Idea. You will know the Big Idea because that will be the red door with the big brass knob right in front of you. That will be the door to open. You will know it.

If you start off writing about your father, write everything you feel about him. Stay in that room until you feel you have nothing left to write, until you are done. Before you rush out of the room, slamming the door behind you, take a good look. Notice everything. Write it all down. Once you have opened the door, you owe it to yourself to write about it all. Some writers call this freewriting, but to me all writing is free, without cost or price. All writing is freedom.

Pushing Open That Door

I like the image of opening the door, even if it is not so original. Some writers write about turning the key and that writing is the key to everything. I like the image of a tour of a house because it seems to fit for me. I like it better than the birth image I have read a lot about in books on writing. I gave birth three times to three large boys, and the images of those long hours of labor and delivery are extremely painful. Not to mention how I looked during all of it.

Open the door because it is not locked. Allow yourself to walk through your past in your mind and to record it on paper. Open the door because there is no secret password, no single-framed eye peering back at you and deciding whether or not you are worthy to enter, as in some 1920s movie mobster speakeasy. Or some roped-off entranceway to a select New York disco in the 1970s.

The door will open to the truth if you let it. Write down what you see along the way. Be open to the possibilities of letting your story help you to heal. My former roommate Laney Katz Becker told me after writing her first novel, *Dear Stranger, Dearest Friend*, that the writing reawakened vivid memories. In her fictional story about two women, their friendship and their breast cancers, Laney, who herself is a survivor of breast cancer, said when she was writing the chapter about chemotherapy, she felt a tingling on the top of her head. The writing was so real for her that she physically felt the sensations she felt during her chemotherapy.

Writing is that powerful.

So many students in my writing workshops have told me that there was one key thing I said in a workshop that helped them to write what they needed to, urged them to open the door. One student said it was when I told the class I cared deeply about the stories they had to tell. Another student said it was that I told her to write in spite of her fear. I hope you find your keys to writing in this book.

What I do in my workshops is offer people permission to write, permission to open the door. I give them the idea that it is OK to trust that behind the door is not a blank, brick wall or an empty elevator shaft or the dud date. I give them the idea that opening the door will lead to healing.

So go ahead. Open the curtain. Open the door. You will find out what is there when you begin to write.

Exercises

1. Close your eyes. Imagine you are in a room with the person you wish to write about or are experiencing the event you need to write about. What

does it feel like to be there? What words do you need to say? How does the place look? How does the person look? What emotions arise for you about this person or event?

2. Write about the most important room in your life. Before you open the door you are anxious to open, do this warm-up exercise. Think about one room in your past or in your present. Is it a room in your future? Was it a classroom? Your bedroom as a child? Is it your office or a therapist's office? Is it the dining room of your home? Is it the basement where you spend time on hobbies? Is it a hospital room or a nursery? Imagine what it feels like to be in this room and write about that. Write every detail you can conjure, take a rest, and try to remember more.

3. Write a list of special places in your life and what it felt like to see those places for the first time. Was it when you walked through an entrance, opened a door, or looked up as you rounded the corner? What did it feel like to see that place for the first time? Were you relieved after so much anticipation? Were you surprised or disappointed?

This essay ran in the *Chicago Tribune* in late 1997. It is about my imaginary friend when I was growing up and the imaginary friends of my children. I named my imaginary friend Betty Sally because I loved both names so much I couldn't decide which one to pick. Betty was the name of my mother's good friend, a woman with eight children who was tall and elegant and wore pearls and slim cocktail dresses to my parents' parties. Sally was a name I liked because I thought a girl with that name would be approachable, likable, without pretense.

On another level this essay is about having permission to be creative and original, as I was granted in my house growing up. Just as I am urging you to open the door to your writing and your creative possibility, I was given permission as a child to act out my imagination. I became sure then as a parent not to diminish the power of my own boys' imaginations and to encourage them to believe in the glory of their creativity.

Where Imaginary Friends Are Always Welcome

Betty Sally lived in the basement, the best part of the house. She looked just like me, except for her long, blond hair, Rapunzel-length. I had a pixie cut. I danced with her in the basement on Clinton Place, and she was never demanding or surly, always ready to play or defer to me. She let me go first at everything from hopscotch to jumping rope and jacks. Betty Sally certainly didn't cajole me into making her bed by saying she was timing me, like one of my sisters did.

I loved Betty Sally deeply, loyally, and fearlessly. When my five older brothers and sisters would tire of me asking them to play, she was forever the willing partner. My mother fixed her snacks and reprimanded my brothers for sitting on her when she came shyly to the kitchen table, often unnoticed. At dinner each night, my father dutifully asked how she was, prompting some melodramatic response until one night when I was five or six I replied that she had died. Pneumonia, I think, or tuberculosis, maybe polio.

When we perpetuate tales of elves, angels, and even a red-suited benevolent old man, I am reminded of the fantasy I built for my childhood and how well it served me. No one told me not to believe in Betty Sally, even if she did get blamed for many of the treacheries I committed as a small child. For she was real to me, real enough to see and smell and touch. I needed her to exist as much as she needed me. She was everything I wanted and needed her to be.

When my oldest son, Weldon, was three, he had an imaginary friend named Shelby who lived in his armoire, the one I whitewashed and tinted a pale blue. I absentmindedly closed the car door on Shelby many times and forgot to set a place for him for dinner, but I never told my son he wasn't real. I remembered Betty Sally. When Weldon was almost four, and we moved back to Chicago near family into a house large and full of promise, I asked where Shelby would sleep.

"I don't need Shelby anymore," he responded matter-of-factly. "I have all my real cousins now."

Between preschool and kindergarten, my second son, Brendan, concocted a boy named Jimmy, a rough-and-tumble type who would not let Brendan make his bed. Jimmy had long lapses in the hospital with various afflictions such as the "toucan pox" (chicken pox was too plain for him) or "monia" and was even paralyzed briefly but recovered in time for a game of tackle soccer, Brendan's favorite.

I listened to the tales of woe—mostly very gruesome involving blood and gore and broken bones—that accompanied Jimmy's Dickensian life, daring not to question the sanctity of his existence. Eventually Jimmy expired one final time, Brendan unwilling to resuscitate him for another romp in the backyard.

Now each night at dinner, we all listen to the travails of Michael, Colin's best friend. Colin, who is three, travels to Michael's house "all by myself," does homework with Michael, and plays basketball with him on a baseball team where they score goals. Michael can be blamed for everything from smearing toothpaste on the cabinet to making too much noise in his room at night. But like all other imaginary companions who have graced the landscape of this family, Michael suffers his share of maladies. Currently Michael is on vacation recuperating from the time his head fell off.

I celebrate the hope I have had, the hope my children have for an inseparable friend who is everything we dream. I am awed by the majestic insistence of imagination allowed to roam, and the strength of a child's fantasy undaunted. I know that each time Shelby, Jimmy, Michael, or Betty Sally has been injured is a reflection of a reality that has stung each one of us. Miraculously, each friend survives the blows, a testament to the resilience of a child's soul. I am as careful to ask the condition of Michael as I was with Shelby and Jimmy, knowing that how well they attend to this friend will be how well they care for one who is real.

I laugh when I see the boys' classmates wearing miniature electronic pets on colored ropes around their necks with beeping reminders to feed them. In the stores, I am amazed at the price tag of these devices and how many people clamor to buy them. Our imaginary friends served the same purpose, without all the bells and whistles. I am glad my children have chosen to have a priceless friend whose life is as simple or morose as whim requires. I am grateful, too, that they eventually will be retired, resting in the peace of a memory that is glorious and undisputed, a fantasy that was just allowed to be.

chapter 7

With or Without Noodles

When I am most inspired and the writing just flows, afterward that sense of having "channeled" from some other, higher source is deeply healing for me.

—France, Writing to Save Your Life Workshop participant

It's OK to Cry

You simply cannot be the mother of three small boys and not at some point have had to defend the health benefits of crying, mostly while said sons are rolling their eyes disgusted that their mother is crying or they are trying so hard to hold their own tears back. I have discovered that sometime between a boy's sixth and seventh birthdays, on the time line of important events following learning to ride a bike and catching a large fish all alone, small boys find it woefully disdainful to cry. They would rather have a bowl-shaped haircut, eat raw broccoli instead of french fries, and be kissed by their mothers in front of their friends while she coos, "Ooh, Snookums Baby, you're my Lovey Precious." But they would never want to cry openly or even admit that they weep in private. One boy who cried throughout first grade was discussed nearly every night at our dinner table.

"Crybaby" is a terrible curse, perhaps the worst one of all in the litany of ancient, traditional childhood curses.

On the other side of the tissue, I am a walking faucet. I can cry at water polo matches if my niece's team is losing, a department store white sale, or the post office if the new stamps so move me. Watching the summer 2000 Olympics televised from Sydney, Australia, I cried at nearly every event, as well as at Olivia Newton-John's triumphant opening song.

I wailed at Megan Quann's surprise gold medal in swimming, for her as well as her parents and how happy they must be. I cried when the U.S. men's gymnastics team blew it big time. I cried for the Chinese gymnasts and the African swimmer who came in long after everyone else. I am perennially on the brink of a tearful jag. I am not faking. I am not doing it for attention. I am just not afraid to shed a few and to show I feel bad.

Sometimes what I write makes me cry. Sometimes when I read what another writer wrote, I cry. Sometimes what you write will make you cry. But you need not avoid writing for fear of dredging it all up.

So many of us have been politely admonished not to dwell on something if it makes you sad. We are told that tears and sadness are to be avoided, as if they are toxic, as if the tears that fall on our cheeks will somehow harm the skin.

If what you need to write and explore in your own words makes you cry, then go there slowly, but do go there. Edith Wharton wrote in 1925 in *The Writing of Fiction*, "In any really good subject, one has only to probe deep enough to come to tears."

Making Noodle Salad

In the Oscar-winning movie *As Good As It Gets*, there's a wonderfully well-written scene where Jack Nicholson is sitting in the backseat of a rental car that Helen Hunt is driving. Greg Kinnear is in the passenger seat, and the trio is on the road trip from hell to meet his parents so he can ask for money. Never mind that the deeper premise of the movie gives me the shivers: a young, gorgeous, funny single mother falls for a creepy, hateful, age-spotty neurotic who is only civil when medicated. But in this one hilarious scene, they're all three in the car comparing life stories and musing that everyone must have had a bad childhood. Jack Nicholson vehemently disagrees.

"It's not true," he says. "Some of us have great stories, pretty stories, that take place at lakes with boats and friends and noodle salad. Just not anyone in this car." He pauses. "What makes it so hard is not that you had it bad but that you're that pissed that so many others had it so good."

I don't think what motivates us to write about our lives and to feel a response to our words is an imaginary checklist comparing our histories with the lives of others, because we can never be as happy or fulfilled as the family across the street. We imagine they are not in their bedrooms at night crying, while they in turn are imagining we are not in our bedrooms crying. I don't think what creates our sadness, anger, or fear is the noodle salad at other people's picnics. It's how we see our own lives, whether or not we had pretty stories with noodle salad ourselves.

We need to write our stories, with or without noodles.

I actually have an aversion to noodle salad. It's always too oily, the noodles are far too squishy, and once I learned the popular recipe calls for the use of frozen peas, I never liked it again. "Tarzan peas" Colin calls that kind because the brand features a green fellow in a version of a loincloth that looks like Tarzan to him.

I also don't like the Hawaiian salad that occasionally rears its ugly head at parties, also known as ambrosia salad, with the marshmallows and the coconut, the canned pineapple and the artificially red, sugary maraschino cherries. These are the same cherries, the same exact ones, that swam in your kiddie cocktails thirty-five years ago. They have a shelf life of three hundred years.

I was watching a morning news show the day after the Emmy Awards were announced. I was trying to get dressed, make beds, supervise the brushing of teeth and hair, and make sure that each boy went to school wearing underwear. Sela Ward was talking about her award for the TV show *Once and Again*. She coolly explained the show's popularity is because people like to laugh and they like to cry.

We don't want to be numb. We want to feel.

You want your writing to help you feel. If you do it honestly, it will. And sometimes you feel like crying. So go ahead.

Letting Yourself Go

You need to write about the tough parts, the parts you don't want to touch with your words. I understand you don't want to remember some of this, you would rather move on. But to anyone who has packed up and moved a household, you know that moving on requires finishing your old business.

You need to register your new address with the post office and all your credit card companies. You must arrange to close accounts before you launch new ones. You need to shut off your phone, electricity, gas, and water before you start up new utilities at your new address.

When you write down your feelings and insights and describe your own story, you can turn on the lights in your new location. Give yourself permission to write what is not polite—what may make you cry.

Crying is OK. Crying can be a release.

I'm not saying you have to make yourself cry or that the only way to heal is to make yourself consistently hysterical or chronically upset, crisis-hopping in your mind and fixating on all the downer periods of your life. "Is this new book going to be a bummer?" a woman I know asked me one morning as I dropped off Colin and Brendan at school. I told her it was a book about writing. If she thinks that is a bummer, that judgment is hers.

It's not necessarily a bummer to cry. A whole lot of the time I feel better afterward.

Lightening Your Load

The tears can be a letting go, a weight lifted from you, the baggage in the boat that if you didn't heave it overboard would take you to the bottom. Lighten your load. Let the tears ease your journey if you feel they could. Crying is not something you should avoid. It's not something you should be afraid will happen when you write.

There are times when what I am writing is so real and honest that I need to stop writing, breathe, and perhaps cry a little because I feel so deeply. It sounds absurd, but sometimes I get up from the computer and go lie down on the floor. My children don't witness this because I write when they are in school or out of the house, but chances are they would think I was bonkers if they saw me. I spoke to my son Brendan's fourth-grade class about writing one morning, and when one girl asked me what happens when the words don't come, I told her about lying on the floor face-down. Brendan looked mortified. It's as if I need to be grounded, and while the weather isn't always conducive to getting down in the dirt, I have found that getting down on the floor works as well.

Sometimes when I am lying on the floor for a few minutes or so, I start to cry. And I let myself cry. Let yourself. Let go.

There are times in your writing that will reawaken the memories for you so vividly, you will need to stop. Honor those instincts and honor your needs. You are celebrating the wisdom of your own words, so please celebrate your own reactions to those words. Get out of the chair, step away from the computer, lie down on the floor or put your head on your desk, and cry.

Author Toni Cade Bambara wrote, "Words set things in motion. I've seen them doing it. Words set up atmospheres, electrical fields, charges." And words can make you cry. Your own words can make you cry, not just the words to a corny song or a sappy TV sitcom.

Releasing the Tears Inside You

The tears can even be a pleasant surprise.

One evening after dinner, I was with Colin on the overstuffed cantaloupe-colored couch in the living room, the one facing the fireplace. He was sitting on my lap, and we were reading under the velvet comforter. Unprompted he said, "I want to tattoo *Michele* on my heart so you're with me all the time." I nearly fainted from the spontaneous love he offered. I held him close, kissed the top of his head, and told him how much I loved him and how sweet that proclamation was.

I held him, closing my eyes, not wanting the moment to pass too quickly, wanting the raw, unedited beauty of his words to stay in the air as long as possible, the vapor, the memory of what he said to linger, frozen, before it had to evaporate. In a minute or so, he pushed away from me and looked up at me, his lips quivering and his eyes wide with surprise. "For some reason, when I said those words, I wanted to cry," he frowned, dumbfounded and confused.

I guess this was a first for my six-year-old son, who only cried when he was sad or hurt or mad. The only time he knew to cry was when he fell from his scooter or got a sliver from the fort in the backyard. I knew this was the first time he cried when he was happy or emotional. How overwhelmed I was with the depth and sincerity of his affection. I thought to myself that when he wrecks the car as a sixteen-year-old or slams the door because I have grounded him at fourteen, I will make myself remember how this felt.

"Sometimes we cry when we're happy or do something nice for someone else," I told him softly, my own lips quivering. "And sometimes we don't know why we cry. We just cry."

If I could count the ten best feelings in my life, this was one of them. It knocked off a first kiss or maybe one that should not have been on the list to begin with. I held Colin for as long as he would let me. After a minute or so, he steeled himself by scrunching up his face and breathing deeply. Then he asked whether I could make macaroni and cheese for dinner. Of course I said yes.

So maybe Colin wasn't over the crying line yet. Maybe he could still let a few salty ones fall. I will never forget how I felt at that moment, feeling that this beautiful little boy was open and loving and could still tell me about it. How powerful his own words were to him and how this was the first time he knew kind words could make him cry too.

I don't gush around my sons too much, having learned to tread lightly in the territory of my sons' vulnerability from the time I ran out on the field of Weldon's T-ball game when he was hit by a ball on the leg. Or the time when I laughed when Brendan told me about a girl in his second-grade class who had a crush on him and stole his baseball hat. So just then, I didn't get too wimpy or call Colin snookie pie or any of that. I just tried to remember every detail of that moment before I let him go.

And I certainly won't tell him I told you about it in this book.

God forbid I should ever tell his older brothers.

Exercises

1. Write down the five big things in your life that have hurt you, made you upset, fearful, or sad. What comes to mind first? This is not about trying to be negative or dwelling on parts of your life when you have felt bad. This is about what you are holding on to that makes you feel agitated or down.

2. From this list, pick the one event, remark, or phase that seems the most important to you. Write everything you can about this one topic. Why is this so upsetting? Why do you feel deeply about it? Can you write until you have cried through it? Is there a way to explain it to yourself? Instead of trying to avoid the feelings, write through them. Are you angry about it? What is the next step? How can you resolve this feeling?

3. Write down your plan of how to deal with this emotion or hurt. Will you speak to a professional counselor, a friend, a clergymember? Where, how, and when can you begin the recovery? Is there another person involved? Would talking to him or her make you feel better or worse?

4. Now write about how it will feel to recover from this feeling. Can you picture yourself not carrying this feeling with you? Write about how it would feel to let the sadness go. Honor the tears inside of you. Let them out. Do not judge yourself for your reactions. Just let them happen.

This essay ran originally in *West Suburban Living* magazine in July 2000 in my "Last Word" column. I was trying to be funny about feeling sad. I poke fun at the public tears of celebrities while also exploring how often I cry and why.

Cry Me a River

I never thought of Bruce Willis as a crybaby. But there he was in my bedroom turning on the faucets, bawling, sobbing, weeping, sniffling, and making himself a generally teary mess. I had rented him and Michelle Pfeiffer for the night and in one particular against-type-casting scene from *The Story of Us*, Mr. Moonlighting Macho was acting like an Italian mother at her oldest son's wedding.

Lately I've seen a whole lot of crying going on.

In the last several months, I have witnessed more public displays of distress than ever before. And it isn't just us girls dabbing our tear ducts at the movies. Men, women, and children have all joined into the collective public sorrow. I won't even mention the relatives of Elian Gonzalez, though it was all so unnerving I would not have been surprised if Janet Reno burst into tears as well. OK, I would have been mildly surprised.

You can expect a smattering of sobbing at the theater, but someone is always crying on TV. I am proud to say I have never seen *Jerry Springer*, but I gather that most people are crying on that show because they've been very recently injured. I don't watch soap operas and haven't for years, possibly since Erica on *All My Children* was on her first TV husband and first Emmy nomination.

But I think I recently noticed water in the eyes of Frank Gifford when Mr. Kathie Lee told the world how his tabloid-splashed, one-hour affair had changed his life. Or maybe it was just makeup in his eye. The next thing you know Al Roker will be wailing during the weather, carrying on about thunderstorms in the East or tornado warnings in the Midwest and what they mean to him. Rush Limbaugh might break down and sob during a Sunday morning harangue on the right to bear arms.

People are crying all over the place. Trust me, I'm not being judgmental. I can cry at a McDonald's commercial if the lighting is just right. I most definitely can't make it through thirty seconds of an ad for the comfort of cotton before I begin to weep. All that visual family togetherness—along with large hamburgers with special sauce or clean sheets drying in the sunshine—gets me every time. The lemonade commercials they run this time of year almost as often as the spots for weight-loss centers are ripe for weeping too. Show me a grandparent on a front porch, a few adorable little giggling kids, a puppy, and I'm a goner.

I think it's a good sign that at this point in history we are all in touch with our inner hysteric. We are no longer humiliated by a shriek and an eruption of emotion. You can be sitting contentedly in a Borders sipping a latte and skimming through recipes for carbohydrate addicts or emotional prescriptions from Dr. Phil McGraw when somewhere in the aisles between psychology and travel, you detect the beginnings of a crying jag. A few people will look up from their short-story collections, but most will pretend not to notice and will continue their search for this month's book club selection, convinced it is as impolite to call attention to a loss of emotional control as it is to tell a stranger his zipper is down.

This openness to our own individual wailing has an odd twist. The paradox is that the more sensitive we are to our own feelings, the more desensitized we get to others' feelings. So here we go, rightfully feeling we have permission to cry like babies in the drive-through or the shoe repair shop. But we turn the other tear-stained cheek when we catch a glimpse of our neighbor doing the same.

I don't know why this happens, but for someone who has cried behind the wheel on the expressway hundreds of times whether it's because my favorite song just started—or ended—or I know I have to make dinner when I get home, everybody else in the universe looks the other way. It is as if by crying out loud you have bared the spinach in your teeth or paraded in public with toilet paper trailing from your shoe. You can cry like a river, but the universe will whistle and hum as they cross the bridge over your troubled water.

Bruce is not alone. A whole bunch of us are crybabies. Especially me. But if and when I see someone else fall over the emotional cliff and let loose with a river of tears, I usually offer tissues. A good cry will clear your outlook the way a few spritzes of Windex and a splash from the garden hose do to your outside windows. You can see more clearly when it's over. Crying is just cleaning your windows.

So go ahead and have a good one. You can use my sleeve. And please, if the moment moves me to tears, let me use yours.

chapter 8

What's So Funny?

Writing keeps me alive.

—Sarah, a writer and mother of two

Questioning Our Reactions

A baby polar bear is very upset and anxious one day and asks his mother, "Mom, am I a polar bear?"

She seems surprised and answers, "Of course you are, dear. I'm a polar bear, your father is a polar bear, your grandfather is a polar bear, your grandmother is a polar bear. We're all polar bears." She smoothes his fur and he rambles away onto the snow and ice.

The next day he asks his father, "Dad, am I a polar bear?"

His father answers gruffly, "Why, of course you are. You come from a long line of very proud polar bears. Your great-grandfather was king of the polar bears. Your great-grandmother was queen of the polar bears. We are all polar bears, Son, and have been since the beginning of time. Why do you ask?"

The baby polar bear responds in a small voice, "Because I'm freezing."

I heard this joke at a dinner party recently and laughed out loud. Someone told it at an outdoor anniversary party for a couple I know. I had gone to this party alone, feeling a little nervous and self-conscious. When I arrived, I knew only two people there. Sitting at a table with great food and all-new faces, on an August night that was warm but not hot and the breeze was cool but not swift, the laughter was a welcome friend. Because it was a good joke. We all laughed.

Everyone I tell it to laughs out loud. I think it's the funniest clean joke I have heard in a long time and it's funny for a specific reason. We all question our own reactions. We all question who we are because we think we're not supposed to think or feel or react in some way, and if we do, there must be something wrong with us.

A polar bear is freezing simply because it's cold. Even if none of the other polar bears look or act cold, he's freezing. And he knows it. He has to trust his own responses. May we all be like the baby polar bear and claim what we're feeling, even if it is unlike anyone else's reaction.

Laughter Is Contagious

If on one side of the writing coin is tears, then the other side must contain laughter. And you can allow yourself not to contain the laughter, but let it loose. Because when you let the laughter go, it spreads. Remember that laughter is contagious. Just ask any preschool teacher.

You may be blessed with a sense of humor—and if you are, you know what a gift it is—and you may be able to see humor in almost anything. You know how you react to something, and you know instinctively how to find humor in almost any situation. Whether or not you think you should laugh or find something funny, you just do. It is not irreverent or disrespectful; it is honest.

Poet and author of the feminist novel *Fear of Flying*, Erica Jong wrote in *Fear of Fifty*, "Writing has often been accompanied by terror, silences and then wild bursts of private laughter that suddenly make all the dread seem worthwhile."

You will find room for laughter in your writing. Or it will find you.

I'm not suggesting you greet each new day in a delirious state of idiocy, refusing to acknowledge the seriousness of a situation. But try to find a laugh. Levity will help. Levity means "a lightness." A lightness of being. A light, an illumination. Allow yourself to see the good. And try to write something that will cheer you. Write something honest and funny, even if it's a reaction you had that struck you as amusing. This isn't about finding humor at anyone else's expense. This is about allowing yourself to laugh when you need to. Just as you need to honor the sadness inside of you and write about that. Honor the yucks.

My family is big on this. My brothers, Bill and Paul, are hilarious. At parties, they can break off into imitations, songs, jokes, anything short of pratfalls. They do accents, strange voices, stranger characters, ad-libbing. They play off each other. My mother's wit is sharp and she could always make us laugh. My father had a laugh that was deep and soulful and warm. He was a great audience. My sisters are funny.

My sisters and I try to get together every other month at a local salon for Sunday massages, manicures, or pedicures, and we talk about everything we can fit into an hour or two. Sometimes we bring spinach dip. We try to solve family problems, talk out issues, and laugh. A lot of it is about the laughing.

This doesn't mean we're like the sister side of the Marx brothers and act goofy around each other constantly. This means we love, enjoy, and honor the spirit of laughter in each other. What we love about each other is not about telling jokes. What we love about each other is that we celebrate the joy in each one of us.

What I don't find funny is self-effacing humor. I never find it funny when comedians talk about how fat they were or how unpopular or how mean their husbands were. I never find it amusing when comedians make fun of themselves in a way that is cruel and self-deprecating—why they weren't loved, why they were wronged. Phyllis Diller and Joan Rivers never struck me as funny. Roseanne was never funny to me. Not only did she put herself down, but she dragged everybody else down with her.

Being a victim isn't funny. Making someone else a victim isn't funny. I don't find celebrity roasts entertaining when everyone shares jokes about one person. Usually it's embarrassing and spiteful. Vengeance isn't funny, but honesty is.

When I was young, Norm Crosby was a comedian who was always on the variety shows. His routines were about words. In a thick Brooklyn accent, he would fracture the meanings and pronunciations of words. Audiences loved him. I loved watching him. His words were funny.

Your words can be too.

Laughter as a Cure

I couldn't live my life without the occasional gift of laughter. It would be like trying to live without ice cubes. Sure, you could do it, but don't some things taste better when you drink them very cold? Isn't water better with ice cubes, and soda? Life without laughter is like trying to live your life lukewarm, room temperature. Sometimes you need something to jolt you awake. A good laugh. Even a smile will do.

Sometimes when I am stressed from work, worrying about money, the boys, complications, deadlines, or my mother, I say to myself, "I need to laugh." It is so deeply a part of who I am. I really need to laugh, maybe not every day, but as often as I can. Just as Gene Kelly sang "Gotta dance" as he swooped across a wooden dance floor so effortlessly, I gotta laugh. It all just seems too hard otherwise.

"Laughter is the best medicine" is an old saying that, unlike many old sayings, is true. Author Norman Cousins wrote about laughter after recuperating from heart surgery. To improve his health, he watched Three Stooges reruns. Personally, I don't find the Three Stooges at all amusing, but I know that millions of fans do. It seems to me like a lot of falling down and a whole lot more hitting, whacking, and getting mad at each other. I see enough of that at home with my own three boys.

Pratfalls aren't funny to me. Perhaps it's the mother in me, but I worry about bruising and broken bones. I never laughed at Chevy Chase when he fell down on *Saturday Night Live*. I didn't think Chris Farley was funny when he fell all over the stage in deliberate attempts at buffoonery. I don't laugh now at the character of Mary Katherine Gallagher who is also falling down and hurting herself on the show. Perhaps I take it all too literally and I need to lighten up, but I worry about them hurting themselves. Someone else's pain is just not funny to me.

But words can be funny to me.

Reading good, funny writing that surprises me, is outrageous, and is original does it for me. I can laugh at the wit and insight of other writers. Calvin Trillin is always funny. Dave Barry is intelligent and wry. Fran Lebowitz's humor is as dry as a Nevada desert. P. S. Wall is quick and has a charming, southern humor I love. The same with Marion Winik. I grew up laughing at the newspaper essays of Erma Bombeck.

Just Gotta Laugh

Sometimes you gotta laugh.

If you can look at a situation or event in your life and comment on it in a way that is honest and real and even funny, then you are leaping toward healing. That shows you can put a spin on it, look at it from a different place, see it in an absurd light, and acknowledge that to laugh at it or with it is OK.

Keep laughter and smiling as an option. Tell yourself in your writing that you are opening the door to good memories too, ones that will transport you somewhere wonderful and happy. Even if nothing strikes you as amusing now, keep the door open. Access the part of you that is joyful.

You don't have to be a comedian. You only have to allow yourself the elasticity to laugh. You can stretch out a laugh and pull back to seriousness. I don't believe we are here to consider our lives as dire episodes of suffering. Nor are we to consider our lives as one joke after another. We are here to consider our lives. And there is laughter in our lives, if we search through the particles of sand to find it. Like gold-rushing prospectors, we can sift through the silt and mud and rock and find pure gold. Laughter is pure gold.

"Happiness depends upon ourselves." I painted Aristotle's words on the breakfast room wall in green paint. I surrounded it with painted ivy for emphasis.

When I was in my teens, my mother bought a sketch at an art fair called *Jesus Laughing*. It looks a lot like the traditional Catholic grade-school image of

Jesus with the long hair and the beard—Ted Nugent but with a kind face. In the drawing, he's about thirty, his head is thrown back, and he is laughing. Who knows at what, perhaps it's one of those Saint Peter at the pearly gates jokes or one of the hundreds of the "A priest, a rabbi, and an atheist were sitting in a boat . . ."

My mother loved this sketch. I liked it far better than all the dire, gruesome images that were and still are scattered about the church we went to every Sunday morning for Mass. I bet Jesus did have some laughs. He's perfect, after all. And human. We are all allowed to laugh. Laughter is divine.

Finding a positive, uplifting side of what you are committing to write about may feel forced and insincere to you at times. I agree that so many things in life are truly not funny. When a hurt or event is fresh or new, it's impossible and inappropriate to laugh about it. But wait. Time may give you the perspective to find something uplifting or worthy of a smile in some part of it. Perhaps it was the gesture of a nurse at the hospital or a note from an old friend expressing support. It could be kindness from a stranger. It could be a memory that grows into a smile.

The world is filled with the possibility of laughter. Just go to an Irish wake and see people with their arms draped on shoulders and smiles as wide as Montana. I'm Irish, and I remember my father's wake, where my good friends came to offer support and all my cousins, aunts, and uncles were there. Of course there were tears. But we laughed about how good my father was and celebrated that we all shared him in our lives. Life is often about duality. Where there are tears, a smile is waiting.

What's so funny? Almost anything can be. If you are honest and unafraid to see the lighter side, you can write to find the laughter. And it can fill you.

Using Humor to Cope

In a scene from one of my favorite movies, *Steel Magnolias*, Julia Roberts plays a young woman with advanced diabetes who will have a kidney transplant the next day. Her mother is donating one of her kidneys to her daughter. The family is at home playing charades. The young woman's two brothers are telling jokes about the operation. "Is it *A Tale of Two Kidneys?*" one brother asks. They all collapse in howling laughter.

Sometimes life just is. It isn't always what you want it to be; it rarely is perfect or predictable. But it can contain a smile because you can put it there. Fantasize, write something outrageous. Exaggerate. Pull at the truth like softened caramel on a taffy apple until the smile sticks to your face. You can use a smile. Humor helps. Humor totally helps.

When my mother had a minor stroke in 1995, she was undergoing surgery to have a section of her carotid artery replaced with a Gore-Tex sheath. The six of us, my brothers and sisters and me, were all in the Columbus Hospital waiting room together. We were nervous and tense, pacing and scared. My father had died six years earlier of complications from a similar stroke. We were all reliving that. We were all scared both our parents would be gone. We were hurting, feeling afraid for our mother, afraid for ourselves, afraid for our children. Afraid of the loss and the grief to come.

After a few hours, my brother Paul told a joke. And then none of us could stop smiling or trying to top each other. Everyone else in the waiting room may have thought we were insane, but it was how we coped. We knew that night we would always have each other and that we each loved our mother immensely. So we laughed. We cried a little bit, but we laughed.

Snapping the Tension with Laughter

When my mother was hospitalized several times after that for spinal fractures, a hip break, and operations related to her advancing osteoporosis, each of us would visit her every day. Even with our busy lives, our visits would often overlap.

Once when Paul, Bill, and I were visiting our mom in this ridiculously cramped room at Loyola Hospital, a large janitor came in the room to change the fluorescent lightbulb over my mother's bed. He was huffing and puffing and then started to climb the ladder laboriously and awkwardly—it was this small footstool really—and nearly toppled onto my mother as she was dozing on the bed. My brothers and I looked at each other in disbelief and burst out laughing. It was almost as if there was a hidden camera in the room.

Was it really funny? No. But the absurdity sparked the laughter that snapped the tension and the fears. It was a relief, it let the air out of the tires, it displaced the pressure.

It works.

I give speeches regularly before women's groups, civic groups, nonprofits, and agencies. I'm often asked to give humorous talks on daily life. For years I called my series What's So Funny? I've delivered hundreds of speeches by now, with different titles, including "Everything I Ever Really Needed to Know, I Faked" and "The Quickest Way to Lose Ten Pounds Is to Let Go of Your Purse."

Recently I was hired by a suburban church group to speak before the adult education series. Several weeks before the speech, I received the brochure announcing my arrival. It was neatly typed and had an enormous picture of me in the center, looking more than a little like a holy card, the one of a martyr or someone you could pray to because she died a gory, bloody death. "Michele Weldon will discuss 'The Use of Humor as a Tool in Daily Living'" it read. There you go, that sounds hilarious. Can't wait.

I called the program director to ask why she changed the name of my talk. She said because she wanted people to know it was humorous. I told her that people would get the idea it was going to be funny perhaps if the title of the talk was funny.

There was silence.

The Many Faces of Humor

Some people just don't think funny. It's almost like being color-blind, I guess. We all have different senses of humor. Humor has a wide range of acceptability. What you consider tasteless, I may consider hysterically funny. What is off-limits to me may be fair game for you.

I don't like jokes at other people's expense. I don't like jokes that are mean. I like jokes, phrases, and humor that surprise me and that are insightful. You may love the Three Stooges. We may both love early *I Love Lucy* shows with a young Lucille Ball. I love the early Woody Allen movies. I despised *There's*

Something about Mary and hated *Pulp Fiction* even more. I dry-heaved through the shooting parts when it seemed everyone else I knew was laughing.

No matter what your style, I think humor is all about being open to the possibility of laughter. Some people shut that door before they wake up and get out of bed. Try not to do that. Keep the door open just a crack.

Write something that makes you smile. Have a good laugh.

Exercises

1. Write down what makes you laugh. Is it a good joke? A special comedy? Do you like reruns of the old sitcoms or do you like cartoons? Is there a writer who makes you laugh? Now write down why those things are funny or humorous to you. Is the humor spontaneous? Does it catch you off guard? Try to figure out why you smile or laugh.

2. Write down how you will give yourself the gift of laughter today. Will you watch a favorite show? Will you read a chapter from a funny book? Will you call a friend and tell him or her a joke, and ask whether he or she knows any good jokes? Will you read the comics in the newspaper? Can you look at old photographs of a vacation or a reunion in which you are laughing? Can you call an old friend and relive a time when you were joyful or an event that was funny? Sometimes just hearing someone else laugh will make you feel happier.

3. Allow yourself to act childish. Can you draw something with crayons on plain white paper that will fill you up and make you happy? Can you play a simple card game like Go Fish or Old Maid? Can you play a board game or charades with a group of friends? Can you act silly by yourself, put on an old outfit that you no longer wear, and play dress-up?

4. Find the humor somewhere you hadn't thought to look before. Is there a way to look at a situation or event in a new light that may bring laughter? Is there

a funny thing that happened to you when you were young or just recently? Can you write a fantasy of what you will be doing in the best of all possible worlds, with all your dreams coming true? This may make you smile.

This essay ran in the November/December 2000 issue of *West Suburban Living* magazine. I was trying to be funny in this absurd piece about reality TV shows. You can try to find humor by exaggerating or deliberately creating something wildly fantastic. Do you have a fantasy you want to write about? Write something that will tickle you and make you smile. Words have the power to change a mood.

A Family Show about Clean Living

The one-hour TV show opens with the camera moving in through the front door of a well-appointed red-brick Georgian home. The camera moves through the yellow foyer, down the basement stairs, carpeted in durable, neutral berber of course, with family photographs lining the walls on either side of the dark green faux marble railing. There's a catchy, instrumental soundtrack, something upbeat with a saxophone and a piano, undertones of thumping bass and drums for a dash of intrigue and suspense.

Then the announcer comes on—you know, the one with the cappuccino voice who does the *Scream* movie trailers as well as just about everything starring Julia Roberts—and he drawls in a dipped-biscotti latte tone, "Welcome to *Chute*, America's only realistic show on clean living where we explore the depths of one family's laundry room. You'll see everything they wear on their sleeves, plus the insides of every family member's intimate wardrobe. We'll show you unedited and untamed exactly what comes through the chute and what it takes to bring it back up the down staircase. In a moment, we'll catch up on this week's dirt."

I see this as the ratings winner every Monday, no, Thursday night, at 8:00 central standard time. I see T-shirts, hats, *Chute* parties, a long list of *Chute* products and accessories, including coffee mugs, laundry bags, stain sticks, even mouse pads. I see people taking bets in bars on who will throw a color in with the whites and who will put the clothes away in the wrong drawers. Will anyone in the family read the cleaning instructions on the manufacturer's tag before throwing a new item into the swirling cycle? Will anybody care?

If *Survivor* (a show where sixteen antisocial strangers tried to be civilized and famous in infamous uncivilization until only one idiot was left standing) can capture the attention of millions of Americans and strangle it for sixteen weeks, then a real live look at American laundry is not too far off course. Who wouldn't be dying to see what really goes on around another family's Kenmore? Who doesn't need the validation?

Think of the advertisers! Every commercial break will scream for the newest, most improved detergent, spray starch, stain remover, washer, dryer, iron, bleach, hanger, or organizer. Even those dewy spots for cotton would be perfectly placed between close-ups of Mom agonizing over a grape juice stain or Brother grumbling and cursing about the sweater that shrunk in the dryer.

The show can begin on Thanksgiving, just when you'd think America would want to watch a football game from the couch. No, what America really wants to do is watch the laundry someone else is doing as they are placing all the gravy-stained linens in baskets and trying to get the cranberry relish out of Baby's new white smock. This Thanksgiving, America wants to see live, up close, and personal, exactly how Mom will attack the sweet potato smear on Sister's viscose rayon hooded shirt. Americans, and especially the target audience of women, ages twenty-one to forty-five, want to spend the holidays seeing whether anyone irons anymore. This is quality TV, even better than Barbara Walters interviewing Celine Dion or George Clooney.

Of course this is about more than dirt and smut.

The season running from the winter holidays through the May sweeps can touch on all the really important aspects of human nature and the bothersome questions of meaning in the universe, such as: Is a hot-water load spiked with bleach really necessary to get whites white or can warm/warm sans Clorox do just as well while saving energy and the environment? Will Brother ever admit that in an attempt to be helpful he accidentally threw Mom's white merino wool jacket in with the rags he used to wash the car? Will Mom split a seam when Dad impatiently yells he has no clean, gray socks to wear when they are already in his dresser drawer? Who will tell Grandpa that his chinos didn't shrink but that he really gained twenty pounds?

If millions can sit through *Big Brother* or *The Real World,* where the real participants seem so childishly inept you wonder how they could tie their shoes and mug for the camera at the same time, then *Chute* is bound to become the number-one TV pastime. It will leap past Regis Philbin and every cop/lawyer/detective show in the ratings race on every network and cable station available to remote clickers around the globe.

Just think of all the befuddling mysteries this show will solve. We will see once and for all that there are definitely dryer fairies who seize unsuspecting socks and whisk them off to a neverland where they are made into quilts for giants. We will see that every ten-pound infant does indeed generate his weight in laundry six times over each day in sheets, blankets, outfit changes, and burp rags. For all the teenagers who indignantly claim their mothers lost their favorite T-shirts, this show will demonstrate that the teenager never placed said T-shirt in the chute at all, but rolled it in a ball and shoved it under the bed.

And for every adult in a family where at least one person plays soccer, football, basketball, or occasionally breaks a sweat on the StairMaster, there will be televised proof that in order to keep up with the onslaught of clothing for work/rest/play/casual Fridays and holidays, one would have to do laundry thirteen hours each day. This will explain why the dryer is always going on high and there is forever a pile of dirty clothes in the basket to be washed. There will also be proof on tape that indeed the dryer does waltz from one point in the laundry room to another when the lights are out and the humans are upstairs. *Chute* will also respond to the age-old inquiry about accountability: No one but Mom ever, ever, ever cleans the lint catcher.

Perhaps I should work to get this show on the clothesline. First, I need to begin scouting for the perfect family who has the perfect laundry chute and critical laundry issues of separation, temperature, and stains we all face. I'd volunteer for the laundry room to be mine, but I nailed the laundry chute in our home shut after my boys orchestrated experiments to see how long it took different objects dropped from the second-floor chute to reach the concrete basement floor. The last experiment involved a Lladró statue I received for Christmas when I was twelve.

Is your house OK?

chapter 9

Honesty Is the Only Policy

Writing has a transforming, emotional, spiritual element.

—Eileen, Writing to Save Your Life Workshop participant

Dressing for Success

First I tried on the pale pink, short-sleeved blouse. No, you can see my lace bra through it. Then the fuchsia blouse. No, too bright. Who was I going to be today? Who did I want to be? Then the phone rang and I remembered (as I stopped listening to whoever was on the other end asking me for a ride for a child) the chartreuse sweater. Perfect. I could wear it with the taupe suit.

So I hung up the phone, put on the sweater and the skirt that I bought too big but was unfortunately filling out at the moment, and ran downstairs to get the boys' breakfast—probably the Cookie Crisps that the baby-sitter bought, which I am morally opposed to but Colin loves. No time to make egg sandwiches—Brendan loves a bagel and scrambled eggs made with chopped pieces of ham and those yellow, yellow slices of cheese individually wrapped that I am morally opposed to also but they all love, except Weldon, who likes his cheddar sharp.

I was going to a luncheon that day for a large foundation for women, and I wanted to look like someone important, maybe someone fashionable, maybe someone some other woman would want to be like. I don't know who, but someone. Someone I would want to be. Someone I'm not.

Later that morning as I made my way through the lobby crowd of hundreds of women, aiming myself for the long, linen-skirted registration table with the typed name tags and the table assignments under the sign marked "S through Z," I thought I should have worn a scarf, my earrings are too small, look at her, she looks good in pants. I should have worn pants, my legs look fat with these shoes. Or I should have worn black. Black always looks good, powerful, neat, elegant.

A hat. I could have worn a hat. Then I would exude confidence. I have lots of hats that I never wear because they look good in the bathroom mirror, then I suddenly get embarrassed in the car about wearing the hat and throw it in the backseat with the soccer balls and the extra clothes for each boy in case we get caught in the rain, they get too muddy, or it suddenly turns cold. That reminds me, I have to remember to put in sweatshirts. And warm hats for the boys because they're always losing their hats. I love hats. You have to deal with a woman in a hat; she can't be ignored. Who should I be today?

I sat down at the table to which I was assigned, table 117, and the plates with salmon were already there at each setting—at one time warm, but no longer, beside it a dollop of dill sauce, a pile of greens. Arugula. I love arugula. And rice with those chopped-up, post-frozen-looking vegetables and pimiento. That's it. Red. I should have worn red. Red would have been perfect. Stand up and notice me, I am powerful. Red.

The Way We Are

After the vanilla mousse in the chocolate cup and four cups of lukewarm coffee, the program began. Six young women climbed the stairs to the stage and the mistress of ceremonies handed them their awards for essay writing on the future for women. There was a seventh-grader, two eighth-graders, and three juniors in high school. One young woman was beaming, her smile about eight feet high projected on the two oversized screens flanking the stage.

"We congratulate these women who have shown the power of writing."

We applauded madly. I felt downright stupid.

Here I was, forty-two years old and not being who I was, not wearing my own power. They were teenagers and more at peace with themselves. That morning I wasn't even sure who I was.

There are days like that, but I hope not too many in my writing. I need to remind myself to be who I genuinely am in everything I write and do, to be sincere, to be true to myself. I am not a woman in a fuchsia blouse and a hat with a plume. None of it matters anyway. Much.

What does matter is being honest. What does matter most in writing is finding your voice, not adopting someone else's.

Starting from Scratch

I tell my graduate and undergraduate students at Northwestern that in the first week or so of class they all have this Voice. It's an adopted, put-on, fake, actor voice that comes through in all their writing. It's all puffed up and full of braggadocio, a brash, cartoon parody of a newscaster voice, inauthentic, one that does not at all reflect who they are. It's almost always remotely British. It's how they think their writing should sound. It's fake, it's awkward, it's awful.

One of my favorite books on writing is Brenda Ueland's *If You Want to Write*. She wrote it in 1938, before World War II, before TV, before e-mail, before my mother who was sixteen at the time had dated my dad. She wrote words that so perfectly sum up the need to be honest in your writing. Her first chapter is entitled "Everybody Is Talented, Original and Has Something Important to Say." Trust that credo and your writing can't help but be honest.

I say this to my students after I have spent hours reading and grading their homework assignments, trying to be encouraging when what they are writing is stiff and false in a pretend journalist voice and not at all like them.

I am always astonished that the handsome and attractive, impossibly brilliant young group with the bright eyes and the résumés filled with trips around the globe and internships at magazines and newspapers and Web sites try to be someone other than who they are. As if who they are isn't magnificent enough.

"You are talented," I say. "I wanted to hear your voice. Tell it in your voice." And then I remember the pink blouse and my wish for the red pantsuit. We all do it. But let's stop. At least when we write.

We All Have a Story

One of the most intriguing students I ever had in a workshop was an eighty-five-year-old woman named Bessie. She was hard of hearing and sat near the front of the room in a north suburban community center. She squinted at me for the three hours I was there and cupped her hand around one ear and asked me to repeat myself often.

She was endearing and sweet and I loved her questions. I promised my students that I would read up to ten pages of a manuscript they had typed, and I would return it at the next workshop with my comments. I always aim to be encouraging, underline the parts I love, ask them to read aloud, and make gentle suggestions such as "perhaps think about explaining this better here" or "more detail here." Mostly I comment on what I like and leave it at that.

No one needs me to be brutally honest. I know what it is like to submit a story, an article, or a book and have someone return it and tell you it seems unreal or why it stinks. I will not bring Grinch comments to anyone who comes to my workshop. I will hold their writing in my hands, marvel at it, and praise the diamonds in the rough, hoping they keep sifting for the gold inside their words and eventually get rid of the rough parts themselves.

So here was Bessie, who handed me a brown envelope—a very thick brown envelope—at the end of the second class, the second of three. On an old typewriter she had typed almost fifty pages. There were spelling mistakes and words crossed out. You could tell she had written it many years earlier and was carrying it with her, probably handing it to every workshop leader and published writer she ever met. Hoping for validation, I guess. Hoping someone would really see who she is and not just an eighty-five-year-old woman in the front row who has a hard time hearing.

Before I started to read it later that week, I told myself I would stop at ten pages and give it back. But I couldn't stop.

Easing into It—Telling the Real Story

The first several pages contained a lot of apologizing and hemming and hawing and then, on about page five, she lost all pretension. Perhaps she was tired of typing. She started to tell her story honestly. It was a raw, painful story about when she was young and her family was extremely poor and the way people teased her. It was so tender and so present, I couldn't stop. She had been honest, trusting her own words, and they were magnificent. In my critique, I praised the parts where she was without affect, where her writing was honest and unselfconscious. When I told her I had read it all, she beamed. I gave her suggestions and recommended that she try to keep her honest voice in everything she wrote from then on.

Trust your words. They will be magnificent.

In one writing exercise in my class, I give the students about thirty minutes to write. I tell them to take me somewhere in their writing. First I read to them the glorious essay "Pointing East" in the book *Thoughts of Home*. It's an outstanding story about Nahant, Massachusetts, written by Brian Doyle. When you're reading it, you can taste, smell, feel the town in every cell of your body. It's that descriptive.

So now that they are fired up and turned on by the sensuality of the words, I tell my students to take me to a favorite place and write about exactly what it is like. I teach many foreign students. The places they take me I will probably never be lucky enough to visit: Japan, Saudi Arabia, Germany, India, France, Ireland, China, and Korea. Many of the students know English as a second language so in their daily assignments, they may have some trouble with minor details of copyediting and larger details of English grammar. Some students must translate directly in their heads, missing idioms and omitting articles. The miraculous part of this assignment is when they write about what they know with an honest voice, their language is perfect. It is as if they are allowing themselves to be who they are. Their writing after that exercise has authenticity to it. They have found their voices.

Can you tell the truth and be who you really are in your writing? Of course you can. As Natalie Goldberg says in her *Writing the Landscape of Your*

Mind tape of her Minnetonka, Minnesota, workshop, "No one ever died from writing it down."

Write What's on Your Mind

Write it down and be authentic to your true self. Have your own voice, not a voice you think you should have or one of a writer you admire. But yours. You were there. You know what the air felt like and what it reminded you of. Use all of your experience, intelligence, and creativity and write your mind. "I take pen and ink and write my mind," William Shakespeare wrote.

Write your own mind. The words inside you are the fingerprints of your feelings, and they are yours. They are your observations and your history that need to be told in your voice, the voice in your head when you are reading to yourself. Your voice should be reading the words you have written. It should be your voice on the audiotape reading your words, not the voice of some actor reading someone else's best-seller. I always like the books on tape best when authors read their own works. Forget the golden-throated celebrity narrators. They have great voices, but let them read their own books. I want to hear the voice of the writer. Literally and figuratively.

"A poem, a sentence causes us to see ourselves," Ralph Waldo Emerson wrote in 1836. So see yourself in your own words.

"Do your own work," every grade school teacher announces at the start of every test as the students grip their pencils anxiously. Do your own work because you have your own voice. To adopt someone else's is cheating. It's cheating yourself out of the power of your words and your voice. Own your words and be honest. It's really the only way any of this works.

I ran into a small amount of criticism for my first published book—predictable rumblings, really—some saying it was only one side of the story. But how I respond is this: If you are asked where you were born and you say, "Cleveland," you know it is indeed where you were born because your mother told you this and you have the birth certificate and for goodness sake she was there.

Now suppose I look at you all squinty eyed and say, "Nope, no, no, no. Can't be Cleveland. No way. I don't believe you. I know people in Cleveland. They don't say you were born there. As a matter of fact, I heard you were born in Topeka, Kansas. You're wrong."

It's still Cleveland. The truth is what the truth is. You know the truth. Be honest about what you know. And write it down the way you know it. It doesn't matter whether anyone disputes it. It's true to you. You know. It's still Cleveland.

Exercises

1. Take me somewhere. It can be a place that was special to you in the past or is special to you now. Tell me about every nook and cranny of the room, about every quadrant of space outdoors. It does not have to be an exotic locale; it can be your basement when you were growing up. It can be a closet where you hid during hide-and-seek. Think about every detail and every sense—hearing, seeing, smelling, tasting, feeling. By writing what you alone know, you are telling a story that is yours alone. So tell it in your own style.

2. Write down why you need to be honest in your writing. Make a list of what you think will happen if you are honest in your writing. Do fears haunt you? Write that down. Will you feel relief? Name that. Will it be confronting? Name that. There are benefits and results of writing honestly. If you can see that, you will be more likely to let go of the fear of being honest and see the good outcome of telling the truth in your own voice. And if you can name your fear, you can look at it more realistically.

3. List all the reasons why you are the only person to tell your story. Write that it is true. Write that you are intelligent and talented and that your story is worth telling. Write every positive adjective you can think of to describe who you are and why you are the only person to tell this story.

4. Remember to tell yourself you can write, therefore you can write the truth. It's a twist on René Descartes's "I think, therefore I am." You write, therefore you can be honest. Say it to yourself five times today and five times tomorrow. Convince yourself being honest is the only way to write meaningfully.

My father died in 1988 before any of my children were born. For several years after his passing, I wrote about how my father affected my life. In this essay published in the *Chicago Tribune* on Father's Day 1992, when I had only two sons and more than a year before my third son was born, I explored my honest feelings for my father. By examining a ritual we had of giving ties as gifts, I was able to honestly look at how his life and his death touched me. Perhaps by writing about a specific anecdote, ritual, or behavior, you can examine something in your life truthfully and see the bigger picture. I still hear comments from readers about the essays I wrote about my father. I think the impact is there because of the honesty of the words. Your written words will have impact on you when you are honest.

Love Knots

It doesn't take a whole lot of imagination to buy your father ties. Ties are the predictable standby gift for Father's Day, Christmas, or birthdays. But the ties I bought my father were different. They were part of the fabric that bound us together.

For the ten years or so before my father died, I would buy him a tie—at his request—in every city I traveled to on business. Whether I was in London or Grand Rapids, I would stop in a department store or boutique and shop until I saw a tie that I knew he would love. And I was always right. He would send me notes in his characteristic scrawl with brief phrases such as "Love the tie" or "Best tie ever," and invariably he would end the letter with "I love you."

I know this father-daughter stuff is supposed to be complicated, but I never found it so. I never worried about what we'd say to each other. Her was a fortress of warmth. He offered love and comfort in its purest forms. I think Dad was mad at me only once in his life. I was sixteen, and boy, did I deserve it.

In the last few years before my father died of a stroke, his tie requests became more involved. It was almost as if he knew our game would be over soon and he was trying to make the most of it. He would send me a catalog page picturing a new sport coat and ask me to find a tie that matched it.

When a newspaper reporter assigned to write my father's obituary called the funeral home, I was the one in the family who spoke to him. "What was your father's style?" the reporter asked. I responded that he was "dapper." It's an odd little word that out of context sounds stupid.

But my dad was dapper. He wore melon-colored sport coats and custom-made Turnbull and Asser shirts. For all the world he looked like a man who had a miniseries in the making about his life. But for anyone close enough, he was the simplest man they knew. He had style, but more than that, he had substance.

When I think about it, Dad probably didn't like the ties as much as he liked our rapport. He had comparable rituals with all six of his children, each customized for the individual, each a territory reserved for that child. With Mary Pat, it was Monday morning phone calls. With Maureen, it was gifts of pistachio nuts. With Madeleine, it was visits with her and her daughters. With Billy, it was golf, and with Paul, it was sharing details at work. His heart was so accommodating that none of us had to compete for his affection. He loved us all so very well and inimitably.

For the last four years, I haven't had to buy my father a tie for Father's Day. And I miss it. My dad wore ties with orange flowers and turquoise peacocks. It was just plain fun.

I have two sons, neither of whom my father will ever know. I sometimes wish for a daughter to share her heart with her father, the way I shared my heart with my dad. I can't picture either of my sons taking the time to shop for their father and buy him the things he will treasure. Maybe it's because they are so young and what they give now is the wealth of their laughter.

What I hope for, though, is that in whatever form they choose, they take the time to build the kind of ties with their father that I have always known: the ties that bond.

Take a Break

The very act of writing is an expression of self-love.

—France, Writing to Save Your Life Workshop participant

Refueling Your Energy

I know, this isn't supposed to be grueling. Neither is sex, exercise, or eating. But sometimes they can be. Sometimes you need to walk away from what you are doing, no matter how good it feels. You need time and space to regroup and rethink, recharge and build up. You need to give yourself permission to rest.

I understand about momentum, I understand that you may now be feeling stoked about the writing you have done and the writing you are doing. Congratulations. I have pulled my share of almost all-nighters, compelled by the writing I am doing. So I know what you mean.

Yet I have also had afternoons or evenings when I would much prefer to drink tea and read decorating magazines, cookbooks, and paperbacks, lying on the couch under a comforter, the cordless phone by my side so I don't have to move to answer it and acknowledge the outside world. These days are rare: my zero velocity days. I have those days only a few times a year, so I know how luxurious they are. If I were to do that every day, I would need a break from resting. My child-care costs would also be through the roof. And no one in the house could finish a book report or science project. Or eat anything more complicated than toast.

You need a break from the writing. Because some of this—perhaps all of it for you—may really be quite hard to face.

Giving Your Memory a Rest

You need to rest when the writing is real. When what you give are the thoughts and memories you hold deeply, you need to acknowledge that and take a break from it. Breaking your silence and wordlessness takes energy. The words ultimately empower you, but at first, your energy is needed to put the words down. And quite simply, expending energy can make you tired.

When your truth is what you are writing, when it is soulful and honest and not random bits of character here and plot there but bits of yourself and your heart, you need respite from it. You need to rest from the therapy. Even though a one-hour massage is glorious, a two-hour massage can be too much. This is why many psychotherapists have forty-five-minute sessions. It isn't just because that's what the insurance companies will pay for, or because the therapists drink a lot of tea or coffee and have to get up to go the rest room, or because they want to leave you in the middle of a panic attack. They need a break.

You need a break.

Taking a break from the writing is the restoration you need from the work.

If you think of your writing in terms of graphic design and page layout in a magazine or a newspaper, think of it as necessary white space. Ask any visual artist; without white space, images become too crowded and too busy, too exhausting. Too many words on a page and it all becomes a formidable, unreadable sea of gray. Your eyes don't know where to focus.

Write too much for too long and it all gets fuzzy and blurry. The goal is clarity, not word length.

Your memory also needs a rest. It's hard to walk through the past for long. That's why so many people leave high school reunions early. It isn't just the food or the fact that the person you secretly hoped was unmarried and still desperately pining for you is happily married with six perfect kids and can't remember your first name. It's hard to spend the evening with your past and not be exhausted. It's hard to be with your own life, examining it with your words and your honesty and not feel tired.

May Sarton wrote, "Each day and the living of it, has to be a conscious creation in which discipline and order are relieved with some play and pure foolishness." You can't keep at it without some relief. Even pitchers rarely pitch more than two or three innings in a row. You have to rest your pitching arm just as you have to rest your writing arm.

Walking Away

Let yourself relax. Let your writing breathe, away from you. Print it out, put it down, walk away. Let the words settle, just as you would take a cake out of the oven and let it cool before you frost it. Your words need to cool down; you need to cool down.

You need quiet to get the writing done and you need quiet to get away from the writing. When you write the truth, the noise of the words can be deafening. If you have written a secret, just the power of the words on paper is overwhelming.

So rest. It's break time. Congratulations on the work you have done so far. Congratulations on opening the door and daring to walk through the rooms. Kudos to you for overcoming the fear, turning on your power, and squashing procrastination like a big, ugly, black bug in the bathtub.

With a diet I was on recently, I could have a reward meal once a day. This is your reward. Have a massage, read a magazine, rent a movie you've been wanting to see but missed in the theater. Go to a museum or take a walk. Ride a bike. Window-shop. Exercise. Swim. Clean out your closets. Try on clothes and get rid of what you haven't worn in three years. Do something menial and rote, like cleaning the cabinets in the kitchen or wiping out the inside of the refrigerator. Clean the oven. Paint a bathroom. Recycle old magazines. Listen to a tape or CD you haven't heard in years. Hum. Nap. Do nothing at all.

And if you've been faking your way through this book, skipping the exercises and wanting to just read about writing, go back and do an exercise you skipped. This is an earned break. As my sister-in-law Bernie would say, no fake-a-titis allowed.

When you've done the writing you need, refresh yourself and recharge. Time to flip the tape over, take the soup off the stove. Like the factory whistle blowing in the old *Flintstones* cartoons, work's over. It's time to get out of the quarry and go home. Enjoy how far you've come.

Exercises

1. Turn off the world. Can you unplug the phone and let the answering machine or voice mail pick up your messages? Can you take a nap or a walk? Can you go to the local health club and swim several laps? If you are not a member of a club, most health facilities have a trial membership where for one day or more you can try out the facilities. If you have small children, can you hire a sitter, swap with another parent for another time, and get in the car and drive for an hour by yourself to somewhere peaceful such as a park or a lake? Once you decide what it is that will relax you, do it.

2. Take a bath. You can light aromatic candles and place them on the floor near the tub, on the sink counter if it is large enough, or on the rim of the tub. Fill the tub with suds or oils and soak. Bring in a pile of catalogs or magazines that you don't care get soggy, and read. Or just look at the pictures.

3. Call an old friend. Have no agenda of asking for a favor or needing to know something specific. Call someone you haven't spoken to in six months, a year, or more. Catch up on news, transitions, everything you can.

4. Be creative. Before I was a single parent, I found time to paint watercolors. I haven't painted in more than five years, but it's a goal. Is there something you used to enjoy doing that you can go back to? Do you like to sketch, paint, or work with clay? Even if you haven't done this since you were a child, pick up some children's clay in the toy store, or children's finger

paints and drawing paper. Or you can go to a ceramic painting studio where you can paint and decorate your own work, such as a teapot or bowl, tile or coffee mug. Keep building on a theme. For instance, have a goal to, over a year or so, make a complete tea set, painting one cup and saucer at a time. Make a set of dessert plates. Or tiles painted for every season or month of the year to hang on a wall.

I love massages. For the last few years, it has been my private indulgence. I try to have one at least every other month, but would love to do it more often. It is how I relax and how I take a break from the world, including the writing. This essay that ran in the *Chicago Tribune* on October 11, 2000, is about my love for that ritual. Is there a ritual of reward you can develop to honor yourself? You need to take a break from honest writing. Do something you love to do, whether it is riding your bike, having a massage, or renting a movie you're anxious to see.

Touching on a Topic That I Love

It's impossible to rub me the wrong way. But please, go ahead and try.

After decades of inhaling women's magazines and *Oprah* late at night, I have finally internalized the self-help/self-improvement urgings and made the leap to self-indulgence. I am remembering my spirit regularly.

And my spirit wants a massage.

I crave massages the way Tammy Faye craves waterproof mascara and Venus Williams craves a well-placed return just out of reach of her sister. Massages are my oxygen supply, my icy sports drink on an August afternoon, the croutons on my Caesar salad of life. I want them, I need them, I love them.

I am no neck-rub neophyte. Since I was a little girl, I pictured massages as supreme luxury, the way it was in the black-and-white movies for Katharine Hepburn in her white cotton robe and turban. And I wanted in on it.

My massage debut came about twenty years ago. I was so nervous and self-conscious, the masseuse kept insisting I try to relax or she would never be able to get the stiffness out of my shoulders. I think it was a combination of the incense and sitar strains, plus long lapses in the dark when I wasn't being massaged that made me agitated, anticipating where she was and where her oily hands might turn up next. Each successive session, I worried whether she thought I was fat. What can I say? I was in my twenties.

After my first son was born when I was thirty, I had massages every few months because I was exhausted in every ounce of bone marrow and wanted an hour in the dark when I wasn't feeding him. As a new mother, I didn't know who was in my skin, and when the lights dimmed and the waterfall tape rushed into every speaker, my mind raced. I hoped and planned what my life would hold next. And then I had two more sons, and I worried with each quarterly excursion to the masseuse whether she thought I looked fat or old or both.

I'm a different person now. I get in, close the door, take off my watch, my shoes, my clothes, pin up my hair, lie down, close my eyes, and drool. Sometimes I go into such a deep trance that when it's all over, I'm scared to drive home for fear I won't be able to react quickly enough to merge.

My mind no longer races during a massage. My mind pulls over to the side of the road and shuts off the engine. And I never worry these days whether I look fat or old. I am who I am and it's OK because at forty-two years old I'm still younger than Goldie Hawn. And I know that when I was Britney Spears's age, I didn't look like her.

In the dark, at the massage therapist's mercy, I let her fingers do the walking. With every step of her agile hands I can imagine the stress slipping away. There goes my next lecture. There goes my next article deadline. Oops, on the last deep-tissue manipulation on my arms, I erased the soccer schedule. And when she reaches for my scalp, I have forgotten the middle names of my children and what I defrosted for dinner. For weeks after a massage, I remember fondly each moment of it, the smells of the room, the quiet, the calm, the soothing voice of the woman. I remember it in such exquisite detail, the way some women remember their wedding or the first time they made a perfect soufflé. Perhaps it's because when I am getting a massage, I am not doing, producing, working, or performing. For sixty glorious minutes I am an anonymous blob on a table in a dark, quiet room without a phone or e-mail access. It's heaven.

I love a good massage and consider a bad massage an impossibility. It's funny, but that simple, drooling, one-hour respite makes me see myself and my life more clearly. And from where I lie on that table, the view is pretty darn good.

Part Two

Paving the Road with Your Words

Your Best Tools

I would like to write . . . and need the confidence and support to get started.
Any suggestions?

—Cindy, in a letter dated October 7, 2000

Assembling the Toolbox

I'm sure some of my own favorite painting creations would make a professional artist cringe. One still life in my living room is a brightly colored acrylic of a vase of flowers on a table with two mismatched legs. I painted it more than twenty years ago, and I think I discovered in the process that I was not terribly good at painting wooden legs. So I stopped at two legs and was prepared to explain to anyone who asked that the table was one of those ledge tables attached to a wall. Besides, the focal point for me was the red Chinese vase. But no one asked.

The paintings I have made satisfy me because when I look at them I remember the thrill of translating from my mind's eye into the physical world something I could hold in my hand and hang on the wall. My watercolors and acrylics are hanging throughout the house: the self-portrait in bright colors with lots of bold-colored patterns when I was in my Henri Matisse period, the watercolor still life, the botanical sketches, even the pears in the sky I painted after I saw a Salvador Dali exhibit in New York at the Museum of Modern Art.

Several years ago at a party I gave, a guest I didn't know well (she was a friend's date) was walking through the house, looking at all the paintings and, I hope, not looking through all the drawers and closets too. She remarked, "I see you have a lot of work by the artist Michele. Do you collect her?"

Why, yes, I do. I collect everything she produces. But lately she hasn't produced much. I gather she is busy. Or perhaps it is just too hard for her to get ready to paint.

Before I start to paint, I have to assemble my tools. I need to go to the basement and dig out the easel. I need to gather my paints, get the easel positioned just right near the window in the family room for the best light, and have water ready in a container to rinse the brushes. Oh, yes, I need to find all the brushes. I need a cloth rag to blot the brush after I rinse it. I need a sketchbook so I can map out what I want to paint. If I am painting from life, I need to arrange the objects exactly the way I want them.

I need to find the painting clothes to wear so the paint doesn't drip on anything I plan to wear in public. I need to put down a tarp in case I spill some of the water. I need to find the right painting music and put that on the CD player. I need to fix myself a Diet Coke and place the cordless phone in the room with me so I don't have to race to the kitchen to answer it. I need to get a baby-sitter so I can have a chunk of time without the children needing 1,465,798 things.

Organizing the Toolbox

Mentally, I make preparing to paint into an ordeal, as involved as packing for a month in Nepal or training for the high-dive competition at the Olympics, so I freak myself out and declare I can't find the time to do all this setup work. So I have had a blank canvas in my front hall closet for about five years. And the painting stays in my head. I know it belongs on my wall so I can lie on the couch, look at it, tell myself how fine it is and how much I like the work of that artist Michele, and how I will go on collecting her and hanging up her work no matter what.

Writing can be like that. If you let it, you will have blank pages in your closet or your desk drawer for years and never let the words come to life. You will put everything else in your life in front of the writing. Don't.

Don't let the story stay inside you because you say you don't have the time to set up for writing. In this chapter and the one following, I will give you your tools. I will help you set up. I will try to answer your questions so you can't use any excuses such as you don't know where to begin. I will tell you.

With three boys who daily try to stall doing their homework, I know the setup trick. That's why I place big stacks of paper and sixty-three thousand sharpened pencils in the breakfast room where homework occurs. Trust me, "I can't do my homework because I don't know where the paper is" has been tried a million times at my address. I know you're too old for that one, so I will help you with the writing tools you genuinely need.

You can find the paper on your own.

The Big Idea and the Outline

Earlier in this book, you named your Big Idea. You now have a road map to follow in your writing. You will not be expecting to go to Iowa and end up in New Jersey. You have named where you want to go. You need to stay true to it.

To help you from veering off your chosen path, I suggest keeping the Big Idea near you when you write. You may or may not be big on Post-its, but you could write down your Big Idea on one of them and stick it to the side of your computer screen. If you write longhand, you can keep it beside you on the desk. Or you could simply write it on an index card and tape it to the side of the computer or keep it near you as you write.

Big Ideas are crucial. While tangents and free-associating in clusters of thoughts may help you feel more creative and limber as a writer, they will not help you when you have a very specific thing you want to address in your writing. Writing randomly will make you bubble about your creativity and feel all charged inside, but it will not help you address what it is you want to say in your writing. You need to put your Big Idea in front of your face and be true to it in your writing.

Just as in mapping out a trip, outline the main thoughts, feelings, and anecdotes you want to include. These are your landmarks that you need to refer to in your writing. These are the points serving as ingredients to your story. These are the ingredients of your soup.

I think this part of the writing process is a lot like the beginning stages of making good soup. You can hunt around for all the ingredients, pulling this out of the refrigerator, this out of the vegetable basket, that out of the cupboard, but you need to have a recipe by the side of the stove so you don't get carried away and add malted-milk balls to the chicken soup because you thought for a brief, insanely creative moment it might be interesting. Soup is good and hearty when you have thought through what fresh ingredients balance what spices and how you envision the texture and flavor. Sometimes when you add too many things, it becomes mud.

If you add sweet potatoes, do you need cilantro to offset it? If you add celery, perhaps adding green onions and turnips is too much. You need a basic guideline—the recipe—to get you where you want to go. You need your Big Idea and you need your outline. These are your writing recipe cards.

When I was in grade school, my third-grade teacher was a relentless outliner. I loved her as a teacher and found her infinitely more interesting than some of the nuns who would spend most of the time trying to terrify us, it seemed, with their ghoulish urban legends about children who ended up maimed, dead, or unmarried because they succumbed to the predictable evils of cigarettes, boys, or worst of all, disobedience to nuns. My teacher had us outline everything from the history of the Plains Indians to the complex sentences we wrote dutifully in neat penmanship, which she graded with red ink.

Making an Outline

I am not suggesting that you outline your life story in the classic format with Roman numerals, capital letters, numbers, and small letters stacked neatly on top of each other like a tiered Black Forest cake. I am suggesting that you list what you want to write about and keep that with you as you write. This list is as simple as a shopping list and only serves as a reminder of what you want to address in your writing. It can be a list of physical, concrete events or objects such as "camping trip." It can be an abstract list of emotions such as "loneliness," if that is important for you to convey.

How many of you have gone to the grocery store without a list and ended up spending three times as much as when you have a list and stick to it? Cover the ground you need to cover to save your life and honor your history by staying on target. Write everything there is to write about your sister's first piano recital, but don't derail into the reason you are opposed to small-waisted fashion dolls or the plotline of your favorite *Dharma and Greg* episode.

Outlining is good. My teacher was right. No one builds a house by just going along, adding materials here and there, until four walls and a roof are finished. You need a plan, a blueprint, to get you from here to there. Otherwise the story you write will be hollow and incomplete, will fall over, and will not completely honor your truth. You will leave whole sides exposed and the big bad wolf may just come along, huff and puff and knock your house down.

And, as learned by the first two pigs who had to go and live with the smart pig brother in the sturdy brick house, that is not a good thing.

Where Do I Begin?

In journalism, the first paragraph in a story or article is called the lead. I like the image of a lead because for me it implies the writer is taking me somewhere, leading me into a place I am choosing to go. The writer is leading me into the foyer, down the cavern, taking me by the hand across a bridge to somewhere new, somewhere familiar, or somewhere unknown. The writer is leading me in a dance that can be a waltz across a smooth wooden floor, a waltz across a desert, or even a miraculous waltz across water. You are the writer of your story, so you are taking the lead in this dance. You are leading yourself to discover your truths.

The lead is the start of it all. So just start. Is there a sentence you tell yourself over and over when you think about an event or feeling? Is it an explanation? Is it a summary of your journey? "I have never forgotten what it felt like to . . ." Start there.

Will it be easier for you to label your event and get on with it? Write what you may have been afraid to say. "I am . . ." or "I was . . ." A simple declaration may offer you momentum, put the gasoline in your tank so you can keep going forward. Can you claim a truth you have avoided? "I am in love with her." Start there. Start simply. But start.

If you just write the word *I*, you've made a good beginning. Make the declaration be your beginning. In my first book, the first line of the first chapter is "I closed my eyes." What do you want to explain? Write the one sentence that you have wanted to write. Begin there.

Starting with the Spoken Word

You can also start with spoken words from a remembered conversation. Sometimes what is so remarkable about an event, transition, or memory is the conversation that surrounds it. Do you want to begin with excerpts of the conversation you can't forget?

Quotations have such power because they have the breath of the speaker around them. Were you told something or did you overhear something that has stayed with you? Are there words with power over you? Begin with those words in quotes, and work in your writing to explain them and why they are so meaningful for you.

For years I have been interviewing people for newspapers and magazines. In the stories that I wrote around those interviews, I found the most power was in the words of the person I interviewed, not in my explanations, descriptions, observations, or exposition.

During the media frenzy surrounding the publication of the fourth Harry Potter book in the fall of 2000, I was asked to interview J. K. Rowling for the *Chicago Tribune*. The remarkable author is known by family and friends as Joanne Kathleen but was assigned the initials by her English publisher who insisted little boys don't buy books written by women. As she was a single mother who wrote books because that was her dream, I felt great affinity toward her, especially since my three boys were ravenous fans of all her books.

The interview was a telephone conference early one Thursday morning.

Seven other newspapers were hooked up to a telephone in a room in New York, and we were to each ask a question round-robin style. Rowling, whose books at that point had already sold 42 million copies, was to answer all of us one at a time, please.

Interviewing the author of the fastest selling books in the history of publishing, I felt like we were the trained seals in the oceanarium and her words were the small fish thrown to us as rewards. We were all gobbling them up hungrily and greedily, knowing anything offered by the gracious young author—herself quite dumbstruck by her overwhelming success—was deliciously sustaining for us. Her words were our meal. And our appetites were voracious. A quote from Rowling was pure, solid sustenance.

"Since the age of six, writing is all I ever wanted to do," she said to my question of whether writing had indeed saved her life. I was madly scribbling those words hoping that some of her writing wisdom would rub off on me and I could tell it to you. I later wrote the article highlighting her answers because it was her words, not mine, that everyone wanted to read.

Just as I needed her words, her quotes to tell her story, can you begin your story with the gift of someone else's words? Can you begin with a quotation of something you said, a line you told someone to explain yourself or an event?

Quotations are real gems, so uncover one and use it as the jumping-off point, the lead to the rest of your story. Is there a quote that reveals a person's character or behavior to you? Can it summarize what you feel? Is it a truth you heard that you wouldn't say out loud? Is there a phrase you heard over and over in your head that marked a significant change in your life?

Other Approaches to Writing

In chapter 6, I wrote about the importance of opening the door and starting to write. In the beginning of your writing, you can begin by showing me what is behind the door. Take me with you to the room where it all changed for you. Take me to a place that is significant in your own life history. Can you use your descriptive tools and show me how it was, as if taking me by the hand?

Another way to begin your story is by telling what isn't true. Perhaps you want to start the writing by showing the irony of your situation and your discovery. Is it critical that you write that you learned how someone or something was the opposite of how it all appeared at first? Can you begin your story with "At first, I thought . . ." and then let me know the truth?

One more way to start your story is to ask a question. "Why did I leave?" And then use the rest of your work to explain the answer. Is there a question you asked yourself over and over when trying to explain the story to yourself in your head? "What could I have done differently?" is an excellent way to begin your tale.

Or you could begin with the end. Write about where you are now and how you feel, then move backward one step at a time to how you got here. Gail Blanke, a friend, creator of her own Lifedesigns workshops, and author of *In My Wildest Dreams*, tells her clients to create a mountain and visualize the top of the mountain as what it is like to succeed at your personal goal, whether it is adopting a child, writing your story, or moving to a new country. Name that as the destination and work down step-by-step, asking yourself, *What happened right before that?* This method helps you to rethink the chronology, even though you are writing it in reverse. You will then have a map of how to get to your destination. But begin with the present and where you are now.

You have to start somewhere. Pick one of the options. They're all valid. They all are ways to get the story out of your head and into a physical space where you can examine it. Start the story whichever way you choose. Write.

Exercises

1. Make an outline of what you want to write. List the points, topics, and emotions you want to address in your writing. The process can be as simple as writing each idea on a line of paper. The list can be one page long or several pages. Be specific, but not so detailed that each topic or idea is limiting. Be careful not to be too broad and write "sadness" or "relief," but relate each to why or how you felt that way in one short phrase. Keep the outline near you

as you write. Pay attention to it; it's your recipe for writing.

2. Decide how to begin. You have many options when choosing the lead for your story. Will it be a declaration? Will a quotation, snippet of a conversation, or remembered phrase spoken by you or someone else be the perfect way to begin? Is there a truth you learned or irony you uncovered that you can use to begin? Open the door and start your story by letting your words lead you through the door and into a scene. Take me to the top of the mountain and tell me how you got there.

3. Stay true to the Big Idea. Keep your Big Idea in mind and near you as you write. Refer to it so you don't get bogged down with other details and other distractions. Read your Big Idea aloud when you begin to write so you can stay focused.

I started this essay, which ran in the September 1999 issue of *West Suburban Living* magazine, with a quote. I was writing about the complaint of boredom I hear from my boys. Starting the story off with the actual spoken words seemed to work and lead effortlessly into the rest of the essay. This story shows how even with all the tools and distractions at your disposal, nothing may be satisfying until you decide to make it work. In this case, my children created their own tools for diversion. Find what works for you as a beginning of your story, gather your tools, and use all of them in your writing to make the writing work for you.

Bore Is a Four-Letter Word

"I'm bored."

Say that to me and you may as well pull off my fingernails, play me every Wayne Newton CD ever recorded, or pour apple juice on my head and ask me to sit a few feet from a nest of wasps. A nest of angry wasps.

I have not found two words in the English language as irritating or as expensive. Whether you are entertaining small children, teenagers, long-lost friends, cousins, siblings, senior relatives, co-workers or out-of-towners, very little in life gets in my craw the way this declaration of dependence does. It implies that whatever you have to offer is just not enough. It implies that even in your splendid company, there's nothing to do. And it implies having nothing to do is a bad thing.

Take my children. In a home filled with so many electronic toys, games, computers, and gadgets that we blow a fuse every few hours, my boys are at a total loss if their agenda goes blank for eleven minutes or more. Never mind a library bulging with books they have never read. Never mind beds that need to be made or clothes that could be sorted.

"I'm bored."

I ask them to explain the feeling of boredom to me, since boredom is such a foreign concept. I explain to them as they stare blankly that in forty-one years I have deliberately chosen not to fill a moment with despair just because it is unscheduled. So what does it feel like to be bored? I ask. The intentional irony is lost on them, the way Beatles lyrics are also lost on them and the humor of *South Park* or *Family Guy* is lost on me.

So we get in the car and drive somewhere to eat something, watch something, play something, hear something, visit someone. We go to a play, festival, show, concert, flea market, fair, race, zoo, museum, arboretum, aquarium, farm, or stable. We attend every event listed in the events section of the local magazine within a twenty-mile radius of our home. About $100 later, we go home.

"I'm bored," they chant in the car, exhausted, with the mustard from the $8 hot dogs still clinging to their cheeks. They sigh and moan, sounding like the children in Dr. Seuss's *Cat in the Hat* who claim there is nothing to do with the mischievous stranger in the red-striped hat they let in the door when their mother left them home alone unsupervised for the day. She is the same mother who, if she left them home alone all day today, would have her children removed from her home by the state.

Boredom is the malaise of the new millennium. Never has there been so much to do on-line or in person. And never have more people proclaimed there was less available to keep them interested. Attention spans have never been shorter and expectations have never been higher.

"I'm bored," they chant.

We go home to rake leaves. They get bored after four minutes of throwing each other in the leaves and go in the house. Wash the car, I suggest. Sweep the porch. Do your homework. Nah. What was I thinking?

And then it happens.

One child finds if you hold your arm to your face and blow on it, it makes an extremely loud, gross sound. They all laugh hysterically. They are enraptured, amused, consumed with joy. Body noises! Why didn't I think of that?

And for the next seven hours, they proceed to make body noises in the confines of the living room, exploring each skin surface—knees, stomachs, backs, legs, arms—with the bold thrill of a New World explorer seeing land for the first time in months.

I walk upstairs and do some of the 372 items on my to-do list and end with reading a book. And as the symphony of body sounds from downstairs reaches a crescendo, I thank God there was at least one chunk of their otherwise unfulfilling day that didn't inspire the loathsome B-word, the very same syllable that grates on my nerves the way explicit rap music or bland Mexican food does. And I pray, loud enough to be heard over the din, that this same glorious activity that consumes them today won't bore them tomorrow.

chapter 12

Getting Where You Need to Go in Your Writing

Writing gives me a sense of peace and a sense of accomplishment.

—Nancy, Writing to Save Your Life Workshop participant

Write in Order of Importance

"Mom wants to know what happened."

In telling a complicated story, you need to imagine you are telling your mother, father, or best friend a long story over the phone. I tell my students at Northwestern and in my workshop this same tip: If you want to know where to go in your story after you have begun, pretend you are telling your mother.

For instance, if you are calling your mother to tell her there was a fire in the movie theater, but you are home safe, you will not torture your mother with the details of how you were trying to decide what to wear to the movies and what movie you would see, about waiting in line and the long process of trying to decide over a large, buttered popcorn with salt or a large box of Raisinettes with a Diet Coke.

Not wanting to infuriate your mother, who is anxious because she knew you were going to the movie theater and the news of the fire at that same theater was just on the 10:00 P.M. newscast, you will start with the fact that you are OK. You won't tell your mother the story chronologically because she will scream and pant and likely disown you until you get to the point.

Write in order of importance. I have a friend who tells the world's longest, most tedious stories. I love him dearly, but I am always finishing his sentences and asking him, "So then what?" I have been accused of severe impatience, but if he is recounting the moments after the pilot announced they have lost an engine, I don't want to hear about the bag of peanuts he put in his briefcase for later.

The STW Rule

"So then what?" This is what I call the STW rule of writing. It may seem to you simply a way of telling the story in the order of how it happened, but it is not that simple. Tell me the story in order of its importance to you. If you are writing about what it felt like to survive that fire in the movie theater, I first want you to tell me whether you are OK. Then I want you to answer the question "So then what?"

What I want to know next is perhaps who was not OK from the fire and what happened to those people who were not as fortunate. After that, I want your writing to answer for me my question "So then what?" Perhaps the next thing is what you feel about being one of the people who was lucky and not one of those who did not survive. That is very different from telling the story in a linear way.

If you can ask yourself after each paragraph, *So then what?* you will know exactly where to go next in your writing. There will be a flow to your work and it will be natural. When you write madly, quickly, and go back to read your work, you will notice the gaps are the spots in your paragraphs that don't easily answer the question "So then what?" Put the paragraphs in the order that answers the question.

The Ham-and-Eggs Detour

You sit down and start the writing, and you get flooded with all sorts of memories and feelings. Some of these are pertinent, but some of them are just the flotsam and jetsam we have floating in our memory that can't really help us get better. Writing is like opening the closet you haven't cleared out in years. You are looking for the ice skates but find the Halloween costumes. Don't start trying on all the costumes right now. You need the ice skates. So find the ice skates. You can go back later and try on all the Halloween costumes.

Write about those feelings that jump up, but don't get derailed by them. Don't go off on what I call the ham-and-eggs detour. Don't start writing in excruciating detail about what you had for breakfast because all of a sudden it seems a little too real to write about what it felt like when your father told you his family secret. Make a note of the other thoughts that occur to you and set those aside for possibly your next Big Idea.

For any of you who have taken writing workshops before or have enrolled in creative writing classes, this may seem foreign to you. The point of this writing is different than the point of other writing you may have done. You are not here solely to exercise the writing muscle. You are here to perform a pointed catharsis, to use the writing as catalyst for something specific you want to explain, expunge, or celebrate. You want to explain something to yourself, not prove to yourself that you can form beautiful sentences about Chilean sea bass.

It is not so much about how you write—though you want your writing to be eloquent and meaningful—as it is about what you write. So make what you write count. I will help you as much as I can with the how. You supply the what. The what is the whole enchilada.

Performing a Clichéctomy

Which brings me right up to the brink of discovery at the dawn of a new era where ships pass in the night with cautious optimism and our thoughts are as dead as doornails.

Don't ruin your writing with clichés. The content is valid, but it can be undermined with clichés. What you have to say is original: what you feel, what you think, what you have experienced has never happened in exactly the same way to anyone else. So why write about any of it using phrases that are as boring, old, and tired as clichés?

Phrases become clichés when they are used over and over verbally and in writing, when they lose their freshness. I had a student once who asked me to give him a list of clichés so he would be careful never to use any of them. The reality is there are far too many clichés in the English language—and in all languages—that you cannot possibly list them all.

There are more clichés than needles in a haystack, but you know what they are. If they are not new to you, if they are familiar and you have read or heard them hundreds of times before, the words form a cliché. Stay away from using someone else's phrasing to describe your unique experiences and your original truths.

"Clichés are quick phrases which once were fresh and shining, but have lost their utility," wrote John Chancellor and Walter R. Mears in *The New News Business* in 1995.

When someone tells me a story with clichés in it, I simply stop listening. It's involuntary because I think I have heard all of it before; my listening mode clicks off. Honor your life with writing that hasn't been done. You are better than that. The phrases you create from your unique set of thoughts and memories will be true to your own history. Use your words. Don't use anyone else's.

Mixing It Up

There are writers I revere, such as Jane Hamilton, Elizabeth Berg, Alice Walker, Tom Wolfe, and Maya Angelou, whose writing is like music. The writing is full of different notes, pauses, and lyrical phrases, not the same droning beat. When you write, try to make your sentences varied. This is my "I Shot the Sheriff" warning. Almost thirty years ago, guitarist Eric Clapton had a hit song, "I Shot the Sheriff," with those words repeated over and over and over again. It had a good beat and you could dance to it, but writing it over and over again would be tedium.

So don't start every sentence the same way, with a noun followed by a verb. Use description and detail to illustrate your point and write about exactly what something looked like, felt like, sounded like. Don't write the same tuna-fish-sandwich sentences. Occasionally write a Reuben with corned beef, Thousand Island dressing, sauerkraut, pickles, Swiss cheese, and rye bread. Served hot.

Every year I go into the classroom of each of my sons and offer an hour or so of writing instruction. I have been doing this since my oldest, Weldon, was in kindergarten. In each class, the students are eager and breathless and always know what they want to write. Sometimes they write me notes to thank me afterward. One girl in Brendan's fourth-grade class wrote, "I can't believe all the words that came out of your mouth about writing . . ." I cherish that note.

At first, I started out having the kindergarten students give dining reviews of the lunches they had just finished. When Weldon was in sixth grade, the writing assignments got more complicated. By then the assignments were fantasies or descriptions of pages I had ripped from decorating magazines. A few of the metaphors used in those classrooms are worth repeating to grown-ups.

The Big-Elephant Analysis

I tell the classes of the younger children that their stories need to be like an elephant's body. In the parable, blind men try to describe to each other what an entire elephant looks like after feeling only a certain part of the whole: a trunk, a tail, the skin. You need to describe all elements of your story in order to give a complete account, an accurate picture of what it was like to you at the time.

Of course, your elephant needs a body. This is your Big Idea, and you already know what that is. But your elephant needs legs to stand on too. Those legs can be recollections, conversations, explanations, and anecdotes that all hold up the Big Idea. Otherwise you are just boasting and claiming something without backing it up. And the elephant will fall over, a big torso with no legs to stand on.

An elephant, naturally, needs his head. Your writing needs to have all the senses covered. Write about what something looked like, smelled like, sounded like, tasted like. Write about what something reminds you of, because as we all know, an elephant never forgets. And that's an intentional cliché. The tusks of the story are the pieces of brilliance, the priceless insights you offer in your writing because your words are pure and original and you know your story to be true.

And your elephant needs a tail. That would be the ending of your story, the natural conclusion to what you intended to say. It doesn't have to be a neat, tidy summary, an Andy Rooney ending, the "That's all, folks" closing lines in his *60 Minutes* oral essays. But offer yourself some resolution of where you have been, where you have gone, and what you will do. Don't just stop writing because you are out of paper. Honor your story with a closing. Bring the curtain down on your writing for now, complete the mission, and honor the Big Idea by fulfilling it.

A Feast of Words

I tell the older students, those in third or fourth grade, that good writing is like an elaborate meal on a buffet table. It can be the salad bar of a restaurant or the complex, block-long buffet at one of those all-you-can-eat chain restaurants. Your writing should not just be bowls of iceberg lettuce after bowls of iceberg lettuce or bins of mashed potatoes followed by bins of mashed potatoes. Write about everything you can think of that pertains to the Big Idea and write it in different ways with conversations, explanations, observations, and anecdotes to give it context.

Your writing can be varied, balanced, and interesting. Write an appetizer of clear, distilled quotations, followed by a main course of an explanation of your Big Idea and a recounting of an event. Then write a side dish with descriptions and anecdotes. Write different kinds of sentences that are sustaining and fulfilling, like corn bread and green beans or three-bean salad and couscous.

Articulate this story as well as you can. Honor the experiences inside you in a way that is worthy of who you are. Your story is not as bland and forgetful as miles and miles of turnips in plain white bowls. Your story is as sumptuous and varied as a Thanksgiving feast. Your words should be as interesting as you are. Your story should be told in a way that is deserving of your experience.

Write what you need to say because it needs to be said. Give the elephant an entire body. Make your feast full. Write what you know and what you remember. And write clearly because what you have to say deserves to be written in words that are as individual and precious as your experiences.

Writing Simply

James Kilpatrick, in *The Writer's Art*, writes about the need to write simply in a chapter called "Faith, Hope and Clarity." He uses an example of a journalist who was writing about a company that shipped bananas. Desperately searching for another word for banana, the writer called it an "elongated yellow fruit." If you are writing a description of a banana, call it a banana and not an elongated yellow fruit.

Sometimes we have a tendency to write our experiences—especially if they are painful or hard to confront—in language that is fluffy or convoluted because the truth itself is hard to face head-on. We hide in big words. I do it. Academics do it. Politicians love to do it. And sometimes we feel that if the writing is shrouded in extra words and confusing punctuation, making the writing obtuse, then the truth will not have to be discovered. And we will not have to face it.

The point is to let the truth be discovered by you through your words. Make it a straight and direct path, not one covered in shrubbery and diversions.

In a writing workshop series I gave, a young woman handed me a story to critique. She wrote about something that caused her great pain and humiliation. She wrote in elongated sentences and complex paragraphs that were difficult to decipher. I had no idea what she was specifically writing about, it was so padded with words that were hard to dissect and phrases that were difficult to ingest. She did not name her truth with a clear Big Idea. The emotions were there, but it was so very unclear because I really didn't know what her feelings were connected to, what event or memory she was reacting to. After ten pages, I really had no idea what she was trying to say, but I knew very well she was trying so hard not to say it. So how could writing her own story help her to understand her story?

I told her in my comments that the writing would be more helpful to her if she were more specific. "But I just couldn't put down the exact truth," she told me. I asked her to try and said that writing down the words and naming the truth may be helpful. I hope she did. The point is even if you show your work to no one else, make your writing clear and understandable to yourself. Name the truth in precise words.

I Can See Clearly Now

Clarity is what will help you to see your history. Don't hide behind words that are lofty and phrasing that is hard to comprehend. Don't use punctuation as a crutch to fall back on so the meaning and the truth get lost in the semicolons. Just as you need to be clear, don't be so terse that you miss saying what you need to say.

Tell it straight out. Simply. Just write it down.

I tell my students to not only perform a clichéctomy on all their writing, but to perform a colonectomy. They can say what they need to say in a straightforward, uncomplicated way so the truth has more room and is not dodging the commas and the semicolons. I tell my students that if they need punctuation such as colons, dashes, and semicolons to make their writing understandable, they likely need to write it more simply to make it easier to understand. Commas and semicolons work like traffic cones in your writing. You don't want to swerve around them to get to the finish line. You want to drive straight there.

There is a balance to achieve with simplicity of words and a musical rhythm to your words. Too complicated a beat and your meaning gets lost, the truth becomes too hard to hear. Too simplistic and the truth is tedious and hard to follow because it feels repetitious.

Getting Active

I have a simple exercise in my journalism classes. I ask for two student volunteers to come to the front of the classroom. I ask one to sit on a chair, curling herself into a fetal position, her head down. I ask the other student to do ten jumping jacks. Then I tell the class that the one student doing the jumping jacks is in the active voice. The student in the fetal position is in the passive voice. Then I beg them to remember this.

Use action in your writing. Your words have more impact when the verbs you use are active and the voice is active. Instead of writing what happened to you, write what someone did and how it affected you as a result. Instead of "I was told I was too tall," you can write "My Aunt Mary told me I was too tall." Every sentence you write can be switched from passive to active just by naming who was responsible for the action.

Part of what is powerful about writing in the active voice is it automatically assigns responsibility for the action, not just the reception of the action. Be aware of the power of action in your words, and avoid writing about receiving action passively. It may help you get to the truth and honor your story quicker. As I tell my students, most of life doesn't happen just because it landed on you when you opened the window.

Writing the Talk

The best advice of all is to write the way you talk. You can walk the talk, so write the talk. Perhaps say in your head what you want to write, then just put those words that way on paper. But I speak in those lofty tones, you say. But I use that kind of style, with commas and semicolons. If you want to know whether your writing is clear and conversational, read it out loud. You have an ear for what is natural. You can hear writing that flows. You will know instinctually how to write by ear. It's like playing an instrument by ear.

Does it sound conversational? Does it sound smooth and simple to understand? You want your story to be simple for you to understand when you are telling it and when you are reading it. The words are meant to help you decipher the past. Don't add another step by needing to decipher the words.

I remember the Dr. Seuss book about the lovable elephant Horton, who told everyone to "Say what you mean and mean what you say." It's good advice. If the words flow easily, they will be easier for you to understand. Does it sound like it flows when you read it aloud to yourself?

A good way to get an ear for what is lyrical, smooth, understandable writing is to go to book readings, poetry readings and library events where an author reads from his or her work, a group discusses a book, or a moderator reads selections of a book out loud. Close your eyes and listen to the written words being spoken.

Good writing sounds as if the writer is speaking it to you, telling you a story.

We all know people who can't quite get to the point in a story, the child who mangles the punch line of a joke. But write your own story in a way that is clear and simple. Just tell the story. Tell yourself your own story in a way that is easy to understand and conversational. It's the best way to get to where you are going.

Exercises

1. Practice rewriting clichés. Pick out ten clichés that you hear all the time in your life. They can range from old sayings, such as "The early bird catches the worm," to tired phrases and descriptions, such as "wide as a barn," or newer phrases, such as "couch potato" or "soccer mom." Now rewrite them in the most colorful, effective, and vivid language you can muster. Describe the same feeling or mood in inventive new ways. Then compare the cliché to your imaginative version. Yours will be much better.

2. Write a description of the room you are in right now. Notice everything. Meditate and contemplate the room before you start writing, being mindful of all your senses. Write down quickly what you see, hear, feel, and smell.

3. Now go back and rewrite that description in a completely different way. Can you start it differently, beginning with sounds instead of visual description? Can you come up with all-new words to describe the scene in a fresh, new way?

Not everything you write is in a logical order. Sometimes you have to move it around, in the same way you tell a story to a friend, not necessarily in chronological order, but in the order that tells the story best. I wrote this essay for the *Chicago Tribune* in April 2000 about moving around furniture to best suit my moods and needs. Several readers wrote letters to the editor that they, too, moved furniture and rearranged as therapy. You are allowed to change the order of your rooms as you are allowed to change the strict order of your story. Tell it in the way that works best for you and gets the point across clearly.

Moving On and On

The blue-and-white-striped couch should go against that wall, the white-denim-slipcovered sleeper should go against those picture windows. There, I see the two ivory armchairs should go there. Definitely, they go there. Move the toy box against that wall, rehang the paintings, put the ottoman over there, pack up the Pokémon puzzles for the basement, wash the tablecloth on the round table and place my favorite book of essays on top—for the imaginary spare moment when I can sit down to read them.

I'm moving again.

Not that I am changing zip codes or addresses, but I am changing the tables, chairs, bookcases, framed photographs, and rugs in the family room. Today it's the family room. Next week or next month it could be one of the boys' rooms. It is 3:00 in the morning and I am moving around. Some women exercise or shop, other women garden or eat, still others work too many hours or worry about their hair or nails. Me? I turn the dining room table sideways for a kick. And it makes me feel magnificent.

I guess it's the megalomaniac in me, but I feel deliriously invincible when I can take a nine-foot couch weighing more than a pregnant hippo and walk it from one end of the living room to the other.

Alone in the inky quiet of our sleep-silenced house, I am once again master of the universe, in control of all that surrounds me. The force is with me and it is forcing me to put the end tables at angles facing the fireplace.

Moving furniture is a power surge for me even if the impromptu moving takes hours and I have to stop and rest on the couch precariously and temporarily blocking all doorways, exits, and access to windows. I get pumped up by the thought of shoving a love seat to a new end of the room. Moving the bookcase with the boys' reference books—the children's encyclopedia, the science project guides, the Spanish dictionaries, the history almanacs—to the hallway for an ad hoc library, or swapping the animal-print pillows from one couch for the raw silk pair with the handwriting in French on the other does it for me. This is what flirting with Caesar did for Cleopatra; it's the same kind of power trip without the jewelry or entourage.

Perhaps the reason I am a home mover and shaker is in my lifetime I have read too many decorating magazines, though I no longer find the time to watch decorating shows on TV. Unless I catch a two-minute kitchen segment on *Good Morning America* as I'm brushing my teeth and shouting to the boys to brush theirs, I no longer can spare the moments to watch the televised transformation of someone else's deck or living room.

Still, every so often, when I am overcome by frustration, stress, or melancholy, I make time to switch the mirrors, rotate the tassels on the handles of the cabinets, or play with the placement of the rugs in the kitchen. I resist the Martha Stewart-ish urge to make all my furniture from recycled pencil shavings (I am no pioneer after all), and instead adhere to the style books by Alexandra Stoddard, considering her wisdom on life and valance placement with the same reverence Richard Gere holds for the Dalai Lama.

Just so you don't dismiss me as unstable, I don't move all the time. It's not always predawn. Sometimes I move in broad daylight. You see, I'm not a binge mover. My children don't come home from school each day with a fearful unreliability that Mom may have just put the breakfast table in the backyard or moved the beds to the basement if it has been a particularly trying day. But I do move enough to keep myself sane. What the planning, shifting, huffing, and puffing has taught me is simple: It charges me creatively, offers me a fresh outlook on the same space, and helps me honor the sanctity of our home.

I call it my spatial therapy.

It's also probably not a bad aerobic workout to move a few tons of wood, metal, and fabric every few months. It's cheaper and easier than actually moving into a new house. There is no packing involved or frantic calls to a mortgage company. No change-of-address cards to fill out and no new neighbors to feel out. And I move only what I am convinced will make an impact on my comfort level or current aesthetic need. Which means I never move around the inside of the refrigerator for kicks. Ever. Not even the baking soda.

Several months ago I moved my thousand-ton queen-size bed with the enormous carved headboard from one wall to a perpendicular wall. It was after a late-night ingestion of an article on feng shui containing the warning that the placement of my bed in the coffin position (meaning the foot of the bed was across from the doorway) was not only bad energy but assuredly inhibiting my health, wealth, and happiness. With this dire warning, I jumped up before the midnight showing of *Politically Incorrect* and began the grueling task of inching the bed to a spot between the closet and the bathroom. Two hours later, sweaty and exalted, I fell into the deep sleep of a woman whose energy was now in accordance with the universe.

"Momma, the room moved!" was Colin's discovery in the early morning.

I grew up with the Carole King–inspired notion that romance was supposed to make the earth move under my feet. I get the metaphor. But while a spontaneously repositioned sideboard or a realigned piano bench may not be on par with dinner across from Liam

Neeson or Jeff Bridges, for now, when the spirit moves me, it suits me fine to move the couches and chairs. To me it means I'm evolving, changing, growing, and moving on. My bedroom is not the same as it was six months ago. And thankfully, neither is the woman in it.

chapter 13

Just Get It Out and on the Paper

It takes so much strength to tell our stories.

—Marie, writer and avid reader

Sealing the Deal

Put it in writing. In business and litigation, that is sound advice to seal a deal, legitimize an oral contract, validate negotiations, and make a transaction, promise, or binding agreement. It is no different when you write to save your life. Put it in writing to get it out of your body and on the paper, to legitimize your story and to objectify your experience.

The process of writing makes it real to you and gives your experiences weight, literal weight. You can hold the paper in your hands; you can transfer the weight from within to outside of you. By putting your story in writing, you are taking it from the transience of memory to the concrete, tangible place on paper where you choose to keep it. You have made it authentic.

In her book *Spilling Open*, Sabrina Ward Harrison uses her words and art to express who she is to herself and to better explore her journeys, growth, and transformations. She writes, "I am learning to write and speak of my true feelings for myself, that's how I can let go sooner and love fuller. It's a mixture of speaking up and speaking in, reaching out and reaching in."

When you reach within to get the words out of your body, the process is transforming. The process of writing is a lightening of the weight you carry inside. I have offered you reasons and inspirations to start the writing. I have given you some of the tools to begin your writing and get you further along. Now you need the encouragement to know that the practice of getting your story out of your body is ongoing and that integrating the process of writing into your life brings continual healing.

Revealing the Truth

Keep going in your writing and have your story continuously unfold as your moods shift, your recollections merge, and your insights sharpen, soften, or change completely. "I write entirely to find out what I'm thinking, what I'm looking at, what I see and what it means, what I want and what I fear," wrote journalist and author Joan Didion.

What she means is she is taking a pulse on her present thoughts while she is writing. She writes not only to express what she has mulled over and digested for years but also to understand herself and her world as events unfold. For her the writing is a spontaneous, simultaneous process of articulating what she feels in the present as well as what she felt in the past.

I met a woman at one of my writing lectures recently who said she wrote down her story. She then regretted telling it harshly, so she ripped it up and softened it, rewriting her history to make it more palatable. She wanted to revise the past. Sometimes the truth is not palatable. What she has done is draw the truth back inside her. She has not allowed the truth to get out. She has dishonored the sanctity and dismissed the power of her own, original words.

Your story is not an entrée to be consumed with meticulous sensitivity and judged by a restaurant reviewer. Your story will not be rated by an outsider on a four-star scale. Your story is for you to let out and digest and consider. Do not water it down to make it less spicy and more appealing to someone else. You are not trying to appeal to a broad audience's bland appetite. Your story is not a jar of salsa labeled hot, medium, or mild. If the truth is hot, let it be hot and write it that way. If it is mild, it is mild and needs to be written as you know it to be true. Don't worry about the label on the jar. Just get it out.

Airing the Dirty Laundry

In the election year 2000, there was a lot of talk in the media of how stories "got out," how one candidate leaked anecdotes and details about the other candidate to the other camp. There was the story that got out about George W. Bush's arrest a quarter of a century earlier. There was the story earlier in the campaign that got out about Al Gore's less than noble history as a landlord. We use the words *get out* because stories need to get out of us. We need to get the truth out of our bodies and on paper. It is called airing the truth.

You need to air the truth, not to the country and to the media, but to yourself. Don't worry about the reception and whether or not the story is nice enough and has the proper spin. Don't rewrite it to be pretty or palatable. You can get out the past. You can get out the present.

In the same election year, President Bill Clinton was in New York for a historic meeting of world leaders at the United Nations, where Cuban leader Fidel Castro was also present. Just prior to the photo opportunity that was the largest gathering of the world's political champions in history, Clinton and Castro exchanged words. For days the media speculated on what those words were. What did they say to each other? What did the words mean? What did they get out? The speculation afterward was bordering on the silly. Some reports in the press were that the two men merely exchanged greetings. Others said the conversation was more meaningful. What words got out? The world wanted to know.

What words will you let out? What words will you get out of your body and on paper? It is critical to your healing and your understanding of yourself to get those words out, as critical as it is to know what passed between two world leaders in a volatile relationship.

Different Approaches to Getting It Out

I find it interesting that a person who is well read or a writer is called a person of letters. The letters can mean the letters of the alphabet or they can mean letters as in prose written to another. Author Isabel Allende described to me in an interview once how she wrote her books. The author of *The House of the Spirits, Paula,* and *Daughter of Fortune* begins each book as if she is writing a letter. She gets her stories out that way.

One of my favorite essays on writing comes from Erica Jong, writing in the *Washington Post* "Book World" section on February 9, 1997. The essay is called "Doing It for Love." Jon Ziomek, the head of the graduate program at Northwestern, gave it to me to pass along to my students. In the essay, the author talks about her own "sacred calling" as an author. "I never remember a time when I didn't write. Notebooks, stories, journals, poems—the act of writing always made me feel centered and whole," the author wrote. "It still does."

For many of you, writing may be the way that you have always processed your feelings. For others, it may be new to you. Some of you may be just trying on this practice, hoping that it fits. But know that the writing and the getting it out is helpful to many who are writers and many who are hoping to write. It is helpful intellectually, creatively, and emotionally. It helps you make sense of things.

Life Is Messy—Letting It Out

Jane Hamilton, who has written four books including *A Map of the World* and *Disobedience,* says writing "absolutely" saves her life. When I interviewed her for a story in the fall of 2000, moments before a packed book signing at a small bookstore on the north side of Chicago, she was calm and focused, a wiser version of the young woman I knew in my classes at Oak Park–River Forest High School. "Life is very messy," Hamilton told me. "Writing helps you order your experience and if you're lucky you can find meaning. If you see life as a series of stories, it makes living life lovelier," she said. Moments later she was standing at a microphone reading from her book passages that were as beautifully crafted as a fine Joan Miró statue, one of a young woman with a long, graceful neck.

But you can't admire the words unless you let them out. The words must be your own, and they must reflect your reality and your truth. Your words must hold the power of your experiences, and you must post them outside of yourself.

I was flying to Austin, Texas, recently, where I was set to speak at two workshops. On the crowded flight from Chicago to Austin, the airline attendant was rushing to deliver everyone their drinks. Beverage service, they call it, when they wheel a cart that seems drastically oversized for the narrow aisle and could possibly decapitate a sleeping passenger if he let his head slip a centimeter into the open abyss between seats.

I was sitting and reading at the end of the aisle. Having finished my soda, I was holding up the can to hand it to the attendant who was busy rushing to collect the empty plastic cups and cans from all the other passengers. She grabbed the can and then in a sweep to throw the garbage away, spilled what was left in another passenger's coffee cup down my back.

As it seeped through my shirt (luckily it was black) and my skin got wet, I screeched, not a word exactly, but a yelp. "Oh, it didn't get on you," the attendant assured me.

"Yes, it did, it's all over my back," I scowled in not such a polite tone.

"No, it was empty," she insisted.

My back was wet, my shirt was wet, and her reassurance didn't matter. The coffee got out of the cup. It did. I was not going to let history be rewritten. It was a washable shirt, but I did have coffee on my back.

The truth gets out. It may not be what you wish it was, but it gets out. Your story is what it is. It may be wet, damp, and uncomfortable, but it is the way you know it to be. Don't rewrite the story to make the attendant more careful or the aisles larger and the ending different than it really was. If your shirt gets wet, your shirt gets wet. Don't tell yourself you can't get the story out because it will not be palatable to everyone involved. It only has to be right to you.

Keep going. Keep writing. Get the feelings out as they occur to you. Keep the door open. Get it out of your body and on paper. Get it in writing.

Exercises

1. Review something you have written from an earlier chapter's exercise. Add new thoughts. Without erasing or editing any of your original words, go back and add your comments either in the margins, on a separate sheet of paper, or in a new file in the computer. For instance, in the chapter 6 exercises, you wrote about being in a particular room with someone. Write about what it feels like looking back at your first writing. Are you surprised by the intensity of some of your reactions? Write about that. When you read your earlier writing, does it feel as if you are reading about the experiences of someone else? Write about that.

2. Think about an event that happened years ago. How has your opinion of that event changed from when you first experienced it? Do you have different insights, a new take? Perhaps you can write about how weeks, months, years after something happened your views and feelings have changed about it. This does not have to be your Big Idea; it can be anything from a first date to a thunderstorm.

3. Brainstorm for a few minutes about your Big Idea. Had you forgotten some specifics or recently remembered more details? Go back to your earlier writing and try to come up with deeper details and more explanations. Just list them. My memories come back in layers. If I concentrate, I can always work on focusing on more details of what someone was wearing, what something reminds me of, how I felt, what I was doing at the time, what it was like then compared to now. Our memory banks are not like safety-deposit boxes that you open and there it is, all the contents laid out neatly for inspection. Our memory bank is a fuzzy, gauzy place where some days the light shines in and you can see that corner clearly and some days the light is out. Some days your memory is as bright as if a 200-watt bulb is shining on it. Take advantage of these different intensities of memory and try to recall more vivid details. Write them down.

It is difficult to write about where and how we feel we fail or fall short of fulfilling our dreams. But it is illuminating because in the process of writing and getting it out on paper, we can look at it more clearly. I wrote this essay, published in the *Chicago Tribune* on June 6, 1999, about taking a trip alone with my oldest son to make amends for not being able to spend enough time alone with any of my children. It was the first time I had ever been able to do anything like that—spend time one-to-one with him—and I was trying to take from the experience new lessons on how better to serve him and meet some of his needs as his parent. The trip was healing for us and the writing about the experience was healing for me. Your writing can be healing when you get it out and get it down.

The Gift of Time with a Child

It took being strapped into a multiaxis trainer—terrified in every cell of my being while jerking, pitching, and rolling uncontrollably at the antigravitational whim of a three-steel-ring contraption—to see my oldest son clearly.

Weldon and I spent a weekend together, away from homework, younger brothers, basketball practices, dishes, laundry, and deadlines to go to the U.S. Space and Rocket Center in Huntsville, Alabama, for parent/child Space Camp.

I hope I never lose sight of him again.

The circumstances of our lives have not afforded us the luxury of a one-to-one relationship, which all the parenting books explain you must seek to keep you connected to your child. I recognize the importance of singular togetherness without siblings, but I have been more consumed by the business of our lives—trying to get each boy to every class, game, and activity with minimal hysteria—than with cherishing the moments I could have alone with each of my sons. So I declared it physically impossible and dismissed its significance. I have been in survival mode, out for minimal conflict and making sure each boy grows older feeling safe, content, and well loved.

It's not that I haven't tried. But if I helped Weldon with a book report or science project for too long, Brendan would grow envious, stomping up to his room and saying I never help him as much. If Colin felt the least bit slighted by my attention, he would attempt dangerous stunts underlined by shouting from the kitchen, "I'm cutting something with the really sharp knife!" So I found it easier on my sanity and eardrums to conduct our lives en masse. We all went everywhere together. No one was jealous. No one was left out.

In my pursuit of serenity, I had no idea what I was sacrificing.

For the first time in eight years, since before I had Weldon's brothers, on this one recent weekend from 4:30 A.M. Friday until 6:00 P.M. Sunday, I spent my days and evenings in the shelter of his company alone, listening to him, watching him, seeing how strangers embraced his infectious sense of wonder. Without the distractions of brothers who share his energy level if not the same number of freckles, I could see him for who he is. And I adore him.

On the same multiaxis contraption used for space training that horrified me, he hollered for joy with each revolution, begging to go again and again. On our shuttle mission with Team Mercury, he diligently accepted his assignments and tasks as flight director and then mission specialist, listening attentively to instructions, remembering the smallest details. For a boy who must be reminded a dozen times to pick his clothes off the floor, it was startling. We told jokes, and I was reminded he possesses a better sense of humor than most forty-year-olds I know.

Not since we put up a swing set in the enormous backyard in our rented house in South Bend when he was eighteen months old have I seen him laugh as much, smile as wide, or gasp with such pure, unbridled joy as often. As his mother, I don't think I ever felt as filled up, relieved, or proud.

As we launched the rockets we built from cardboard, glue, and hasty instruction, my spirits soared while Weldon yelped that his had gone a mile high into the afternoon sky. We returned to our cramped dorm room exhausted after fifteen hours of activities that included three trips to the same cafeteria where breakfast resembled lunch and lunch strongly resembled dinner but tasted magnificent just for the company.

But I could never go right to sleep, though Weldon climbed into the bunk bed that was so thin he said the mattress was "made of sand" and fell asleep with only a few remarks about his space station model and our team's mission patch. The first night I cried a little because he was so happy. The second night I cried a little because I didn't know when I would have the chance to do something like this with him again.

In only hours we would be back to our family routine of "pick up your shoes, finish your homework, clear the dishes, get in the car, don't hit your brother, remember your lunch, it's bedtime" that has defined our lives.

The weekend was a generous gift from my sister Madeleine and her husband, Mike, for Weldon's tenth birthday. Although I could never have sought such extravagant adventure for ourselves, I vow to recreate the priceless adventure any way and any day I can.

I know I don't have to fly to Hunstville to find out what I discovered there. I can have an hour of kite-flying with Brendan in a nearby park. I can read a book with Colin, holding him in my arms as he tries to say the words. I can eat dinner on the floor of the family room with Weldon when the other two boys are asleep or at a friend's house. And I can know each of them again, know them well, and love them vigorously.

It's a dream I have, a dream of being the kind of parent I want to be. It's a dream I had at Space Camp. And it's a dream as big as space.

chapter 14

Beyond the Superficial

Writing is healing for me because it gives me a joyful opportunity to be in the creative flow, speak from my heart, and share the wisdom of my years. It awakens my inner voice and sends me on a soul-stirring journey of self-discovery.

—Sheila, public speaker and author

Bringing the Page to Life

For a short time in the late 1980s, I was an interim art critic for the *Dallas Times Herald*. I got to write about exhibitions, acquisitions, even a counterfeit sculptural artifact discovered at the Dallas Museum of Art and a woman in Waco who claimed she had physical evidence that proved Leonardo da Vinci's painting of the Mona Lisa was not of a young woman but of his young male lover. She was colorful anyway.

What I learned in those few months was that I had to use my words to be the eyes for the absent readers and embroider the blank page with detail, metaphors, symbols, and every trick I could conjure to relate what a painting, sculpture, or body of work was like visually. I needed to use my words as if I were describing a sunset to a blind person. I tried in every piece I wrote to describe carefully my emotional reaction and the context of the work. It was hard to do. And it taught me how important it is to use complex, descriptive detail in writing and to abandon forever the cheap practice of using flat, simple descriptions.

Empty words simply couldn't do the job. Knowing that also helped me for the years I wrote about fashion as a freelancer for the *Chicago Sun-Times* and for Fairchild Publications, where I worked for three years as a market editor for *Footwear News*. After a while, a whole lot of the collections, new lines, and "breakthrough" concepts start to merge, unless you pay close attention to describe each as narrowly and carefully as you can. If you are writing about a new line of shoes for an industry whose profits rely on heel heights, toe shapes, textures, and color, you learn quickly how to be precisely descriptive. Shoes, clothing, art: I had to use my words to paint the pictures in everything I wrote. It was great training for later writing about my life.

I remember sitting at the computer on deadline in Dallas trying to give context to some artworks I was reviewing. I was scouring my memory for titles of paintings I saw in my mind's eye flashing *ka-ding, ka-ding* on the over-head screen in a slide show for an A-level art history class I took my sopho-more year of college. It was a "mic" class (short for Mickey Mouse) because word was you could get a good grade with little effort. I took the class with my friend Susan and mostly we chatted about all subjects other than art history during the lectures. Ten years later on deadline trying to make sense out of an art collection, I was wishing I had paid closer attention.

Finding a Fresh Perspective

Superficial words such as *good* or *bad* didn't work. They won't work for you either in telling your story. They're just not enough. You need to move beyond the typical labels to describe meaningfully what something was like for you, exactly what it was like for you. Assigning an event pat adjectives and dis-posable-cottonball words such as *nice* or *bad* falls short of the mark. They are inadequate. Your story deserves better than that.

In her 1934 book *Becoming a Writer*, Dorothea Brande writes about describ-ing with "innocence of eye": the willingness to look at your memories or impressions with a fresh gaze. Brande continues, "Each fresh fact starts a train of associations reaching down into the depths of your nature, releasing for your use sensations and experiences, old delights, old mirrors, days that have been overlaid in your memory, episodes which you had quite forgotten."

Description is vital in writing to save your life. You are trying to convey with clarity and meaning the story you have within. Using timid words that don't explain well what you mean or what you know is like trying to drain a flooded basement one teaspoon at a time. You can't get the truth out fast enough using words that have such limited capacity or depth. Empty words just can't hold enough water.

"Try not to view the subject as you've been taught to view it," author and poet Rebecca McClanahan writes in her book *Word Painting*.

Taking a Good Look Around

Years ago when I interviewed the prolific, acclaimed author Joyce Carol Oates, it was hard to escape the observation that she was busy visually taking in all the details of every aspect of the tiny faculty office at Southern Methodist University. I was speaking to her moments before she was to deliver a guest lecture to a literature class, and as we spoke, she was smoothing her hand over the podium, lifting stacks of papers to see what was beneath, her eyes darting around the room in keen, relentless surveillance. That's why this talented writer of *We Were the Mulvaneys*, *Blonde*, and so many other novels and short stories would never commit a description that was aimless or flat. She notices.

Your experience is more than *awful* or *nice*. Your story deserves to be told in language abundant in specifics, using similes, metaphors, analogies, and symbols to convey to yourself *exactly* what the experience was like. Tell yourself the story with careful, conscious reflection.

When you read something you have written, you should feel as if you are there again. But this time you are taking back control of an event; this time you can articulate what it means and how you felt, giving voice to a past that was perhaps mute.

"If you're writing out of a need to communicate, to hear your own voice on the page, then you owe it to yourself—and to your family—to write," author and editor Jack Heffron writes in *The Writer's Idea Book*.

You owe it to yourself to write in words that are not bulk-mail throwaways. Write instead with words that deeply resonate the truth for you, mirror for you images that are vibrant and whole, three-dimensional holograms that mimic reality precisely, not merely reflect a quick glance in a store window as you drive past.

Write with "Hallelujah Chorus" energy that makes your story ripe and glorious, shining with truth. Try to put into descriptive words just how it was to be you just then, just there, with surgeon exactitude and a hyperalertness.

Design the words carefully, as meticulously as a set designer creating a play's specific time and place, following the direction of the playwright to the smallest detail. You are the designer and playwright.

Close your eyes and go back to the moment. Write what colors are there, what small objects, what large objects, the motion of activity, the smells, the sounds, the atmosphere, the gestures, everything. And describe it in words that are as thick and bountiful as chili with all the fixins: chopped onions, cheddar cheese, chilies, meat, beans, and sour cream. Hold the heartburn.

Through the Eyes of a Child

When he was about two or three years old, my oldest son, Weldon, had a very creative way of naming places and people in his own imaginative verbal shorthand. He called Target the "yo-yo store" because its red logo looks like a yo-yo. He called Sam's Club the "big-ceiling store." Sometimes when we went outside to get in the car for errands, he would close his eyes and say, "It smells like winter." And I would stop and smell, and he would be right. Of course he would also point to people and say his observations out loud. Once he called a very large woman in a purple sweat suit "Barney's mother." He has grown to be more discreet.

Before young children learn it is polite and socially acceptable to be inoffensive, they say what they see in colorful, imaginative ways. They don't know safe words yet and declare their observations in words that are honest and customized for their worldview. What they come up with is surprising and engaging. They haven't learned yet to call something "interesting" or "boring" because when they are very young few things bore them and most everything interests them. When you write to describe your history, go back to that mindset and write with young, innocent eyes that are not jaded, bored, or too polite.

Write what you see. Call it something original and unique to your thought process. Describe a tree, not as a tree has been described six billion times before, but as only you can describe it with your intelligence, your memories, and your brilliant and unusual take on the world.

Use physical descriptions that compare and contrast. Make analogies. Write what the blue sky reminds you of, not only that it is blue. Is it the color of your favorite blanket as a child? Is something else the texture of your favorite blanket as a child? Your memories are not flat and dull, as are the knives in my kitchen that make all my brothers, sisters, and in-laws groan when we try to slice bread or carve a turkey at the holidays. Your memories are sharp and glistening. So let the integrity of your words match your memories.

Fine-Tuning

When I was young—around kindergarten or first grade—the Sunday comics section was the only part of the newspaper I cared to read. It was the only day of the week the comics were in color. Every other day the cartoons were reduced to black and white. In black and white they didn't seem as funny or enticing. But sometimes on Sundays the color printing of the comic strips was out of register, an eensy teensy bit off, the red hair of Brenda Starr a smidgen too high so that part of her cheek bore the outline of a *That Girl* flip. It had to do with the alignment of the image on the newspaper presses, but it bothered me that the pictures were marred and smudgy.

When you use words that are simple and lifeless to describe events that are enormously important to you, the writing is out of register with your experience. The intensity of your writing does not match the intensity of your experience. It's off. Call it back into register and adjust the tracking with words that are pointed and full.

In the late 1950s, writer Duane Best interviewed author William Faulkner at the University of Oregon . The question-and-answer session is printed in the 1989 book *On Being a Writer*. In the interview, Faulkner, the author of classics such as *The Sound and the Fury* and *As I Lay Dying,* said, "It is the personal satisfaction that comes when you ring the bell and know it; when you know you have completely expressed your idea. It is in knowing that you have written the truth."

Ring the bell and know it with words that echo the song of what is inside of you. Make it a song with words that are satisfying because they are accurate reflections of your truth, not something nice or bad or easy. Don't settle for the cheap, imitation words devoid of deep meaning. Find the twenty-four-karat words that are dazzling and evocative.

Your words should be as rich as a chocolate chip cookie full of walnuts, raisins, and three kinds of chocolate chips: white, milk, and dark. Your story is not a simple sugar cookie hastily made of butter, flour, and sugar, pressed into a pan. Your story is layered with scents, tastes, ingredients, and textures of details that move beyond simple description and labeling. The words should reflect the depth of your experience.

Words such as *nice* are what we say about people or places when we feel we have nothing else to say, when our phrasing is listless and we don't put forth the energy to explain something well. You have words of all shapes, sizes, sounds, and meaning at your disposal. Don't limit your words to hollow explanations.

Buy a thick thesaurus and look through it for words when you're writing. A marvelous book to help you find new words is Barbara Ann Kipfer's *The Writer's Digest Flip Dictionary*. Borrow a book of quotations from the library and look through it to see the words and phrases great thinkers have employed. It will ignite some thoughts within you and inspire you to ring the bells of your own story.

You deserve to tell your story. And you deserve to tell it well.

Exercises

1. Review your writing and locate the simplistic, bland words. Circle them. Now above these words, add new words that are more exact and precise. Need help? Look up the original word in the dictionary for its definition or a synonym. If you have a thesaurus in your computer, click on the word and see whether another word comes up. Can you create a metaphor? For instance, instead of writing "the evening was still," write that "the evening was hide-and-seek still" or "boulder still."

2. Review your writing and add more sensory descriptions. There is much more to writing than visual description. When describing a place or person, write down what the place smelled like or sounded like. What cologne was the person wearing? Did the room smell of pumpkin bread that was moist and loaded with cinnamon? Close your eyes and try to recall all the senses of the moment: sight, sound, smell, taste, touch.

3. If you have described an event, don't just write the facts about what happened. Tell how it happened. Write how this person walked, how fast the event happened, how people were talking, how time was moving, and how you were reacting. The how, including adjectives and metaphors, is as important to convey as the what.

This essay appeared in the *Chicago Tribune* on May 24, 1998. It's about trends in new fragrances for women and how downright silly some of them seemed to me at first—especially the scents called "Cucumber" and "Mud." This story is really about noticing everything around you and taking note when the world begins to smell different. A fragrance that mimics a bread-baking kitchen conjures more than just the aroma of the blended ingredients. In your writing, think about what every encounter reminds you of and the details of how it makes you feel, taking note of all your senses.

In a World of Fragrances, All Noses Lead Home

The fig was more than I could handle. Before that, I was engaged, captivated, primed for purchase. The lab-coated saleswoman had been spritzing me for at least ten minutes. I was feeling vulnerable and needy, every commission-craving employee's dream.

"I want a new smell," I implored.

Almost giddy, the charming lady in the lab coat continued her frenzied spraying fest, applying essences of lemongrass, vanilla, chamomile, and green tea. She chattered as she sprayed, describing the irresistible properties of each seemingly edible combination and their remarkable allure for men, women, children, and some small animals. Then she sprayed for me a strip of fig, and that's when she lost me. I walked away with a stack of strips that could attract wasps.

If you haven't noticed, wake up and smell the coffee behind your best friend's ears. The world of women smells different. The new scent of a woman is more closely connected to the kitchen than any other room of the house. A friend recently told me he had read somewhere (OK, so now this is thirdhand) that the most hormonally appealing scent for a woman to wear is the combination of licorice and cucumbers. Gee, think of all the money I wasted on Calvin Klein and Donna Karan scents over the years when all I had to do was rub the sauce for gyros or a few black jelly beans behind my ears.

Women have smelled like floral arrangements or spice gardens for as long as I can remember. Elevators in department stores smelled intensely—sometimes a little too much—like hydrangeas, roses, lilacs, or gardenias. Though I could not be specific about how or why a perfume or cologne was pleasant, it had to do with the feminine, floral smell of our house on a Saturday night when my mother would sing to herself and carry the small purse. It was the smell of an older sister's first date, how she would set her hair in hot curlers, paint on eye shadow, and spray on perfume liberally and menacingly as I would watch from the foot of the bed, envious, speechless, and enraptured.

I remember the baby powder smells of my adolescence while we were trying desperately to act like adults but still smelled like infants. Then appeared the signature scents of my favorite designers, bought more for what was promised in the advertisements than what they actually smelled like. The smells were unidentifiable, mysterious, provocative. It was an emotion evoked, a feeling, a promise of adventure. I could pretend I was as glamorous as a woman on a Milan runway or as unpredictable as a Ray-Ban-wearing heiress running to slip into the passenger seat of a Jaguar.

But now women smell just plain delicious, like sweet fruits, a bowl of bananas and oranges in the breakfast room. They also smell like cookies baking or aromatic soup simmering on the stove. They smell like a lemonade stand in the summer or honey waiting for a thick, porous slice of warm bread. I guess a shortcut to a new aromatic life would be to dab some vanilla extract on my wrists the next time I make banana bread.

I have also taken note that I am beckoned to smell like the great outdoors. I have been given magnificent bottles of a scent called Rain. I have walked through stores smelling of Heaven and Grass. Someone once told me they had smelled Mud, and I reminded them they could stand near my sons on any given Saturday and smell the authentic inspiration for free.

But if I were in the business of marketing fragrances, I would aim for the smells a woman like me craves. Those cravings would take my nose out of the kitchen and into the rest of the house. I love the smell of dryer sheets because that means the laundry is nearly done, the last load anyway. Eau de Fabric Softener Sheet may be a hit for women twenty-five to forty-five, married, with children.

Along the same lines, a fragrance that smells like bathroom cleaner would do it for me. That smell means the bathrooms in the house are safe and that the bacterial hazards of living with three small boys are at least temporarily arrested. Furniture polish is another good, hearty smell that means the living room is clean. A friend once told me she sprays furniture polish in the air before her mother comes to visit. Her mother always remarks, "Your house is so clean." No, she smiles to herself, it just smells clean.

A week or so after my fig encounter, I was still on the trail of a new scent, though I knew I didn't want to smell like a kitchen. I wanted to smell fresh, exciting, and unlike any scent in my fragrance history. I ended up buying a blue cologne in a store where I was more than twice the age of every salesgirl and customer. I wore it out to dinner that night. An hour or so later, I had a red, splotchy rash all over my neck. Maybe I should have gone with the fig.

chapter 15

Take the Dare

Writing helps me organize my world.

—Mary, Northwestern University Medill School of Journalism graduate student

Confidence Is Key

I have a rotten sense of direction. Internet directions don't help. Even with a detailed printout of right and left turns, approximate travel times, mileage, and full-color maps, I have done more than my share of driving in frenzied circles in the coffee-guzzling moments before I am scheduled to give a speech in a city I don't know or a suburb I don't recognize.

So I understand doubt.

In your writing, you are going somewhere new. This may even feel like driving somewhere new in a new car, a stick shift when you are used to driving an automatic. But the difference is that in your writing, you will end up at the destination where you need to go. You are following your Big Idea and your outline, and you are staying on course. You will get there. You just will. Stop and rethink what you want to write and go over your directions. Be confident.

"So much of writing is about confidence," author Anna Quindlen told an audience of close to five hundred recently at the Chicago Public Library for a signing of her book *A Short Guide to a Happy Life*. As the best-selling author stood at the podium in the grand, wood-paneled auditorium where every seat was filled, she continued, "We are all really writers. Some of us for money, some of us for love. I guess it's like sex that way." The crowd laughed. She has the confidence to write with the same spontaneity and eloquence as when she speaks.

Be confident you will get to where you need to go in your writing. You are writing for love of yourself and for love of your words. Please don't doubt yourself. Don't give yourself ammunition for anxiety and say that what you have done is not good writing, that you may have remembered this incorrectly, or that you really didn't want to write about that thing at all.

If you are nervous and a little scared to continue to write what you've been writing, it is exactly what you should be writing about. The big truths are hard to tell. Everybody can write about the first day of school when you are young and happy and make new friends. The stories that are truly consequential, that we must retell ourselves, seem so fraught with doubt and insecurity.

On the first day of every class and workshop I teach, I ask each student to stand, give his or her name, and declare why they are good at writing. So many backtrack, hesitate shyly, and say, "Someone told me once . . ." I interrupt and tell them to make a declaration, a definitive statement about why they are good at this. From the first moments, I try to make my classroom a safe place to be confident. The claims can be anything from "I notice things well" or "I have a lot I want to say" to "I am willing to learn all I can." After each student makes the claim, we applaud madly. Most former students tell me that simple exercise keeps them afloat for months, even years.

It's easy to write about how much you love cornflakes. It's hard to write about the words your best friend said that changed you forever, a trauma that haunts you, or the deepest feelings you have about a parent or a child. It is even difficult to explain to yourself why someone or something makes you deliriously and uncontrollably happy. You have to write about where, when, and why the ecstasy began and what it means.

Don't Second-Guess Yourself

When what it is you are writing taps into your core, you will begin the process headstrong and confident. Then in the midst of things, as the water is lapping up to your knees, you'll start to doubt that writing it is the right thing to do—that you even know how—and try to abandon it all and run to dry land. You will doubt that your writing is correct. But it is.

You may be afraid that you will regret what you are writing. Try to work through those doubts and reassure yourself that if you stay true to your Big Idea and realize it is true, it isn't wrong.

I have said and done things I regret. I have said things I regret to friends. I have said things I regret to my children. I have acted impulsively and out of anger. I do less and less of this the older I get, but I sure did a lot of this in my twenties, though not as much of it in my thirties. I'm still at the dawn of my forties, so I won't make any sweeping generalities about how far I am past all of that. I'm nowhere near perfect.

Yet, so far, I don't regret anything I have written, not the content of it anyway. I can look back on some of my work and wince that this doesn't flow there, that that was not the most lyrical phrasing of that, that I didn't execute the thought as smoothly as I would have liked, and that my writing will never have the brilliance of this writer I admire or that writer whose work I adore. But I have tried to tell my truth in my writing, and I regret none of it.

Don't regret what you have written. If you write the truth, it is your best shot and it isn't wrong. There is no such thing as a wrong answer in your writing. If it is honest, if it is your accurate truth as you know it, it deserves to be in writing. Don't back out now. You have come too far.

In 1960, author Harlan Ellison wrote, "Without truth, my truth, the only truth I know, it's all a gambol in the pasture without rhythm or sense."

In this process of writing to save your life, you may have written words you have not even spoken out loud. You may have committed to paper and put down memories and feelings you never dared articulate. Leave them there on the paper. Don't second-guess yourself and take the words back. No take-backs allowed. This isn't a Pokémon trading-card game. This isn't what my children go through several times a week with their baseball cards and their games of improvised daring in the car.

This is why I urge you to keep this writing private. Publish your stories if that is your goal, but remember the primary mission of this book is to help you to honor your story for you. To use your words to help you heal. Anything beyond that, as a friend of mine would say, is gravy.

And because it was bold and brave of you to write it at all, don't allow someone else to sit in judgment of your history and your truth. This is your life so you know it isn't wrong. You can claim it. You absolutely are right if you are honest with yourself.

"That healing begins where the wound was made," author Alice Walker wrote in her book *The Way Forward Is with a Broken Heart*. Start the writing where the wound was made. Healing begins where your honesty begins.

"Life never presents us with anything which may not be looked upon as a fresh starting point, no less than a termination," André Gide wrote in *The Counterfeiters* in 1925. If you are doubting yourself for what you have written, look at it as a fresh beginning of a new life that honors writing the truth.

Privacy Issues

When I taught a series of writing workshops a few years ago, I'd pick out a handful of works students had given me to edit that I felt would be useful to share with the group at the beginning of each workshop. I'd ask the writers privately whether it would be OK to call on them to read their works aloud. Some works were so brilliant and colorful they made me gasp. One woman's essay was masterful. I asked for permission to call on her. She agreed.

I urged her to be brave. Tentatively, she stood up and read her words, so moving, raw, and tender that many of the fifty or so people in the workshop were silently weeping. It was an extraordinary and beautifully written piece about an extremely personal and intense experience. I thought she had done a remarkable job and that her writing hand was so closely in touch with her heart it seemed as if there was a direct link, an artery from her heart to her hand that was driving her writing, uncensored, bold, and powerful. I stood there beaming like a parent at the school play when her child is the lead. I felt so proud of what she wrote and the courage it took her to claim it.

After the woman sat down, another woman raised her hand and said coldly, "I don't think the beginning was very believable." Everyone sighed. If this had been a less polite crowd, she would have been booed. I glanced at the woman who had been reading, and she seemed visibly crushed. I was quite upset that it was me who had urged her to read it aloud. I dared her. I was now wondering whether that was the right thing to do. I never expected someone in this safe space of a writing workshop to be competitive, hypercritical, or insensitive and try to separate her truth from her words in an attempt to diminish what she wrote.

But she did. I then made a comment about everyone in the workshop being sensitive to others' creativity and about how I thought this woman's work was outstanding. The woman who had dared to read her work still looked defeated. I couldn't save her from the lesson that not everyone will support your writing and your truth. I am trying to save you from that lesson.

Accepting the Dare

The reality is that other people can be critical, for whatever reason. I think those people who criticize writers—whether in reviews, in a class, or verbally in a casual conversation—find it threatening or feel vulnerable around someone who is open to the power of his or her own truth and is available for the truth to come forth in his or her own words. Perhaps they feel it undermines their own courage and urges them to face in their own writing something they don't want to face. They rage "How dare you?" when the truth is you don't know how you dared to do it, exactly. All you know is it has taken all of your strength to dare yourself to write it down.

Please dare. I dare you. And I applaud you for your willingness to explore your own life and utilize the words that you carry inside of you for something profoundly meaningful and healing. I dare you because I dare me, and the daring has helped me grow. I think you are strong for daring to write it down.

Don't let those negative voices, those critics, those people who stand in judgment of your writing get in the way of your writing and cause you to doubt yourself and think you are wrong. This writing is for you. The goal is to heal. Please remind yourself that in writing your own truth, there is no such thing as a wrong answer. There just isn't.

This is not like the science test my fourth-grader, Brendan, takes or the math or science quiz Weldon is madly studying for almost every night. This is not even like teaching Colin to read with a limited number of correct responses for how to pronounce each letter. Those are all finite sciences and disciplines with right and wrong answers and not much gray area. There is no recount allowed. The answers are right or wrong. Period. Some answers may even seem wrong, but are right.

There was the evening I was helping Colin to read when he came across the word *would*. He dutifully sounded it out pronouncing the letter *l*.

When I told him the word was the same as "wood" and rhymed with "hood," he squinted his eyes and said, "Now why would you say that?"

No matter how it looks, no matter if someone says it could be wrong, your words are yours and you are right if you are adhering to what you know to be true. Your life is not a finite, confinable science nor is your memory. The impact of your experiences on your emotions and your attitudes is subjective, and you are allowed to express what you feel and think about all of it. Even if the truth may hurt your mother or your best friend.

So I urge you to keep it private to save yourself the hurt of someone criticizing you for daring to write about it. Work to publish it if you feel you must, but work to tell your truth to yourself first and foremost.

You have to tell the truth as you know it, and once you do, you have to let go of the fear of how it will be received. Allowing yourself to receive and try to understand the truth is the whole point. You are writing to heal, so let the words you write heal you and don't let a critic interfere with that healing by telling you that you're wrong.

Immersing Yourself

I was in Saint Petersburg, Florida, recently for work related to my first book. I had a few hours off from receptions and events so I went down to the hotel's outdoor pool. It was a quiet, old hotel masquerading as a New Age spa. I was alone. The pool was empty because it was early morning, with only a few other guests sitting poolside reading newspapers in lounge chairs.

I took to the center of the pool and started to swim. I lay on my back, doing a gentle backstroke. My ears underwater, my eyes closed, I could hear myself breathe. Amplified, my inhalations seemed exaggerated and clear. I could hear the rustling of the water underneath the surface and the rushing of water from the jets by the side of the pool. As soon as I lifted my entire head out of the water and opened my eyes, I could hear and see the people chattering in their lounge chairs, the women in white terry cloth robes waiting for their nail treatments or rose-petal wraps, drinking coffee and telling stories about books read, elaborate meals enjoyed, and exciting places visited. Back underwater, I was alone with myself and my breathing.

Writing is like that; it is a private, underwater space where you only hear yourself. The world is still out there when you choose to enter back into it. The world is always there outside of what you are writing, but it is separate from your writing. You can temporarily shut out that noise, take respite, and swim beneath the surface, listening only to the music of your own breath and the truth inside of you. And write.

"All good writing is swimming under water and holding your breath," F. Scott Fitzgerald wrote in *The Crack-Up*.

You need to write from that sacred place that only you have access to. You can have your own words and your own truth be what fills you up, what consumes your concentration. You can't stay underwater forever, but you can keep your truth and your words separate from the outside, honored and whole, away from the scrutiny of everyone else. Pay attention to the words that are there, the ones no one else can read or hear. They are yours and they are not wrong. Remember they are not wrong.

On that trip to Florida I met Connie May Fowler, an author of several remarkable books including *Before Women Had Wings* and *Remembering Blue*. She is a talented, intelligent woman with an attitude of joyfulness. She said that she writes to honor herself and that she has written since she was a little girl. "Writing absolutely saved my life," she said. And because she writes from a place of pure honesty, she added, "The material is making me write it."

Your truth will make you write it. You will write the material that needs to be written, when it needs to be written. Trust in that. Go underwater in your writing and listen to your breath and the magic of the truth beating in your own heart.

Exercises

1. Make a list of truths you have dared to write so far and what that daring means to you. Go back over the writing you have done and cull from those words the big truths you dared to say and how that made you feel. Did you feel powerful? Relieved? Did you relive the emotion and become able to look at it more clearly? Did it frighten you to read what you wrote? How can you ease those fears?

2. Make a list of reasons why it is important for you to tell yourself the truth about your life. For instance, you can write that the life you are saving is worth saving or that what you need to tell should be remembered. You may write that writing feels calming or cleansing. You can write that you are taking ownership of events in your life and claiming your truth to make it more real.

3. Write down a list of reasons why you need to keep writing. Does writing down your experiences and insights make you feel more in control of your life? Is it freeing for you creatively, or is it an intellectual exercise that helps you organize your past and present? Have you begun to feel the healing benefits of writing? Take a look at what the writing is doing for you. And write down the reasons why you need to maintain the writing, even after you have explored your first Big Idea.

Courage isn't just about taking obvious physical risks. We don't have to re-enact a scene from the movie *Braveheart* to show that we are brave of heart. Being daring sometimes means only daring to write the truth. It may seem small, but daring to write down your story may change everything about how you feel and look at your own history and future. I wrote this column for *West Suburban Living* magazine in September 2000 as a commentary on people going to extremes to be daring in sports and recreation. It's meant to be a funny look at the latest crazes in sports. To you, writing a sentence of searing truth may be an extreme. I dare you to explore that territory.

Let's Not Go to Extremes

This is a column of extreme importance. This is a column about the importance of extremes. More precisely, it is about how extremely important extremes have become to everyone—it seems—but me.

I'm not talking about being the biggest exaggerator on the block. We all know people like that, whose children and distant relatives are the first in the universe on everything from shoe tying to SAT scores and whose homes grow ten thousand feet per year. I'm also not talking about self-anointed extremists who seem to speak with exclamation points at the end of every sentence, using the punctuation mark I feel belongs only after the words *fire* or *help*. Whether they are describing a ride home or the latest trip to the grocery store, a sense of urgency underlines every breath.

No. The extremes I refer to are supposed to be fun. I'm talking extreme sports, or the pastime of nearly dying for a good time. And I just plain don't get why that would be appealing.

Grown men and women are barreling down the rapids at night with their infants, a week's supply of gorp in their waterproof back-packs—an experience they choose to call vacation. Responsible parents are adhering themselves to vertical cliffs, grabbing on with their fingernails, and asking a friend to snap the photo, which, I gather, is to include with their last will and testament.

Have these people never arrived at an airport fifteen minutes before their flight takes off? Why would they need to recreate the adrenaline rush available anytime you attempt to balance a checkbook? For some reason (call it my survival instinct), I don't consider it a game or sport if I am performing a stunt that on the face of it, is life threatening. I'm not that good a loser.

I guess it would be understandable if all these new daredevil sports were limited to those under twenty-one, before a genuine sense of mortality—or just genuine sense—had accrued. But it's people my age—my age, for goodness sake—out there bungee jumping, hanging on to gliders, diving from mountaintops, and swimming across cold channels.

Yes, I am a fraidy cat. And I have been since I was small. I distinctly recall going to a local weekend festival at about eight years old, climbing confidently into the rocking capsule of the Zipper ride, and screaming to be released the moment the engine started to roar and the capsule capsized into thin air.

I don't find unadulterated terror amusing. It's the same survival instinct that kept me from joining my oldest son on The Twilight Zone Tower of Terror at Disney-MGM Studios. The brochure scared me. Drop thirteen floors in an elevator on purpose? No thanks. I admit now that I take my three boys to the Ferris wheel at Navy Pier and close my eyes the entire time while gripping the hand of my six-year-old, who, I am convinced, will accidentally dive eight stories below once we reach the top.

Life is scary enough. Rush-hour traffic can add gray hairs, raise blood pressure, and shorten fingernails. The way I look at it, driving to work is perilous. Driving late at night seems extreme. And eating out? With recent reports of contamination from unsuspected foods, sometimes you feel as if you play Russian roulette with every order.

Being a parent is extreme enough. Now that the rage of other parents whose children are on your child's sports team can prove fatal, I'm feeling intimidated about this fall's soccer season. I may just wave at my boys as they run past on the field, holding up a sign with a smiley face from the safety of my locked car.

I am an extreme wimp. The black-and-white scene of Miss Almira Gulch pedaling her bicycle to take away Toto in the original *Wizard of Oz* still scares the bejesus out of me. My heart pounds to see her legs circling madly with the menacing "da-da-duh, da-duh-duh" score in the background.

My threshold of terror is in the basement, so I will never understand why anyone would compete in extreme games and live to laugh about it. The most dangerous thing I like to do is guess on Monday nights whether this week's broadcast of *Once and Again* is a rerun. I'll dare to help my sixth-grader with math homework, and I will take a deep breath with every fall thunderstorm that the basement doesn't flood. I'm not an extremist. I make no apologies for not wanting to compete in pushing the envelope. I'd rather lick the envelope and place a stamp in the right-hand corner. It's risky enough to assume it will get there.

chapter 16

Check Out the Flip Side

Writing is cathartic and it helps me remember
people and things in a positive light.

—Molly, Northwestern University Medill School of Journalism graduate student

Sunny-Side Up, Please

Willie Nelson sang a song years ago telling us to "direct your feet to the sunny side of the street." The peppy little tune always seemed to me a little out of character for him—or at least for the persona of who I assumed he was. It was a finger-snapping number that was played in a lot of jukeboxes in the early 1980s. It is a song about optimism, about switching your point of view to the other side where the sun is bright and clear.

My son Colin was looking out the window in the upstairs hallway in the muddled hours before school began one recent October morning. The sky was overcast and blue-gray—one of those mornings you wanted either to shrink back under the covers for escape or have a pot of strong, hot coffee brewing in order to make it through to 10:00 A.M. without yawning or trying repeatedly to skulk back to bed.

"It's a pretend sunny day," he surmised quickly. "It's sunny underneath."

Now here's a worldview I hope he takes with him through life. It sounds dangerously close to that pop-song, sunny-side approach, but I bet good money if he maintains that outlook, it will serve him well through high school, college, goodness knows through marriage and small children, even when his own children reach adolescence and they tell him he's wrong about everything and especially that attitude. I don't know for sure whether he gets this gregarious attitude from me, but I am definitely taking the credit.

In your writing, please remember to explore the sunny-underneath part as well as what is on the surface. Write about both sides of the coin, including the flip side. What compels me to look beyond one simple viewpoint is my journalism background, likely beginning with my journalism professors in undergraduate days who conditioned us all with frank sternness to look for opposing viewpoints, to find balance and fairness.

Striving for Balance

I tell my students that it is imperative to present balance in their articles and essays, to make the picture rounded and full, not flat and one-dimensional. I tell them their stories are like a finely crafted handmade table, which needs four legs to hold it up. Otherwise the table will fall over. You need more than one leg of the table, one snapshot view, one way of looking at your story to be balanced. Try to find another vantage point.

Jill Ker Conway, whose memoir *The Road from Coorain* scrutinizes her Australian childhood, writes that when she first began writing a memoir, all the recollections and images she recalled were painful. In her essay "Points of Departure," published in the book *Inventing the Truth*, Conway writes, "But in the process of telling that story I rediscovered so much that was beautiful about my childhood." She continues, "Often there is a human tendency to obliterate happiness—to live in one's painful memories."

Do not obliterate the other side of happiness in your writing. Seek it out. Write about the joyful memories as well.

In writing to save your life, you are allowed to have different takes on your same truth. Perhaps those opinions and recollections will shift over time with different moods. We are constantly growing and changing, thankfully, and our paradigms shift.

Because you know there is no such thing as a wrong answer, choosing to look at your history more deeply from another angle may yield different writing and make your writing discovery more enriching for you. You may understand yourself a little better and your own story will emerge not just as a simple recap of events, a news digest of blurbs written matter-of-factly as a report, but as a helpful, healing exploration of your past.

Etching in More Detail

I invite you to go back and explore what's underneath, the inside, the other side, the outside, and write about all the feelings you have about an event or memory—the good as well as the bad. But try now to find the good. Try to recall the affirming and the alluring as well as the painful and the raw. You are adding to the writing, not changing it. You are not altering the basic features of the face of your own story, you are merely etching in more details. You are adding smile lines and sparkle to the eyes. You are looking more closely.

Poet Kahlil Gibran wrote, "Your joy is your sorrow unmasked. And the selfsame well from which your laughter rises was oftentimes filled with tears, / And how else can it be?"

I understand the compulsion you may have felt to put your experiences into words. To label them and claim them as your own. It is an empowering act, a bold declaration. I completely understand that writing down what you have experienced mimics scenes from those old black-and-white *Perry Mason* TV shows, when invariably someone on the witness stand would stand up and point to the defendant at the table, sitting sheepishly with his lawyers and shout, "That's him!" You want to point to what has happened and say it in your own words, pronouncing the truth irrevocably.

But writing does not stop there. Keep going back and adding to your writing new insights or different illuminations you may have had since your first writing.

"The events in our lives happen in a sequence in time, but in their significance to ourselves, they find their own order, a timetable not necessarily—

perhaps not possibly—chronological," Eudora Welty wrote in her 1938 book *One Writer's Beginnings*. Struggling to tell her own stories, the legendary writer realized the fits and false starts of her memory's engine. Writing about her family and their frequent trips together, she wrote, "But with the passage of time, I could look back on them and see them bringing me news, discoveries, premonitions, promises—I still can, they still do."

The Great *Aha!*

This practice of going back to your writing and adding all the gray and subtly shaded areas of your recollections and insights will grant you permission to explore the prismatic rainbow of your feelings, not one strict color or one strict view. When you hold a prism to the light, you can see the different colors. When you hold the truth to the light, you can see the different colors it portrays to you.

Writing with this attitude then allows you to further explore the reality you have named. It may even be the first time you take a look in this way and see your experience as a multifaceted sculpture with breadth and weight, not just a flat, single episode without depth, irony, or polarity.

It's like on those cop-and-lawyer shows where in the middle of a tense, dramatic deposition or testimony, the client will suddenly exclaim, "Yes, she was that same person I saw in the red dress at the convenience store buying paper towels at midnight. I hadn't really thought about it before. You're right! She's innocent! She could not have been at the crime scene."

Allow yourself the *aha* of discovery simply by giving your memory another sweep, holding the truth up to the light. You will not retract your declaration, but you may find something new that's uplifting and freeing.

When you look out the window, you may choose to see a gray day that requires a jumper-cable boost in order to face, or you can see a pretend sunny day underneath. Writing the good and the positive as well as the sharp and negative allows you to explore different areas of your experiences. Going back to your work and asking yourself to look at the positive side will likely give you a more detailed version of the past. Your writing will then not just be a simple, quick sketch relating the truth. It will emerge as an M. C. Escher drawing, with intricate shadings and complex subtleties you could not see when you were just trying to get the truth out of your body.

You will perhaps also learn to forgive yourself and your role in your own history. For me, writing my first book and including in it the reasons why I fell in love with my former husband and why I stayed married were extremely important for me. My marriage was not always dark; there were times when I felt sincerely and completely happy. At best, writing the positive and the negative made me see how completely confusing and enigmatic it was to live in that duality. And writing about it gave me permission to see that and helped me to forgive myself—and him. It was an integral part of the truth that I only dared to look at in the writing. And only when I dared to take a different look, less from my wounded self and more from my self that was naive and romantic, could I piece more of my life together and my reasons for acting the way I did.

"The real discovery consists not in seeking new landscapes, but in having new eyes," Marcel Proust wrote in *Remembrance of Things Past*. I am suggesting that you look at your history with new eyes to see what is there for your own discovery. Blink once and look again. There is wisdom hidden in our mistakes and misfortunes, waiting to be unearthed.

Gaining Perspective

We all remember in bits and pieces, snapshots and fragments, not one smooth, linear, chronological movie playing seamlessly. If we think about our memories as split-screen feature films, then we can understand and trust in having different takes on our own past.

In order to gain perspective, some time needs to have passed since your earlier writing. The reason I wait until this point in the writing process to stress the need for balance is because you needed first to work out your Big Idea and get the truth out of your body before you could even consider going back and adding more. You needed to exorcise your truth. I define *exorcise* as getting rid of or letting it out. That was the goal.

I'm not changing the rules of the game here, like instructors in exercise classes who fool you into thinking you are only doing twenty lunges when it is actually twenty at a time, and you end up doing one hundred and have sore legs for a week.

No, you are still driving to your destination with the road map of your Big Idea. You are only now going back into the writing and asking yourself more questions. I am urging you to go back to the driving, not to get to a new place, but to take a better look out the window during your route. Concentrate this time less on the road in front of you and more on the minutiae of the vista you are passing. Let your writing display more of the color of your feelings. It's autumn out there and the leaves are not all the same shade of green.

Writing from different depths of our own history allows us to be more human and less strident in our views of the world and of ourselves. The water has different temperatures the deeper you go beneath the surface. Yet it is still the same water.

I already know what you may be saying to yourself. There may have been nothing redemptive about your experience, and honoring the truth of your Big Idea disqualifies the possibility of finding the positive. There is no other way to view it. It is what it is, it was what it was. Why would I ask you to doubt your own truth and be dishonest to your history? There is no bliss there, you say.

Please look again. Or let more time pass and look then. I am not suggesting you doubt. I am suggesting you add.

I tend to be ruthlessly optimistic, which is why I still have size eight jeans in my closet and have the boys' birthday parties at our house with a white denim couch in the family room. You should see the weight listed on my driver's license. That's pure optimism.

But this is not about conjuring something that isn't there for appearances. This is not about quashing the truth and finding a Hollywood ending that is neat and uplifting. This is about writing about positive aspects of major, even traumatic experiences, as a tool to feel more positive, get through it, and emerge out the other side without a poisonous, bitter taste in your mouth.

Focusing on Your Strength

What may be positive is that you survived at all. Write a declaration of your strength; that is the legitimate, positive view. This writing is about using your words to feel better about yourself and what you know to be true.

When you write down good memories that made you feel whole and loved, conjuring the sights, sounds, and essences of people and places you hold dear, then you feel better. There was some good there. There was always good in you. It is affirming, it is positive, and you can let the words shine for themselves. The words will embrace you and comfort you.

When I write about my children, my family, or my good friends, I revisit the Grand Canyon–size love I feel for them, and I realize how blessed I am. This is not to say each day with the boys is an exercise in delirious happiness. There are arguments, tantrums, slammed doors, and dangerously spiteful words. While raising them is astoundingly difficult, it is preposterously joyous at the same time. By articulating the good, I can see the good more clearly. I can see why I have done certain things and what I need to do better.

Writing what is positive, I can look fondly on people and places in the present and the past as a way to acknowledge the good. It is not saccharine and delusional; it is real. Being positive and writing positive feelings and memories whittles away at the pain, *chip, chip, chip*. It may simply begin to make you feel happier.

"Writing is not life, but I think that sometimes it can be a way back to life," Stephen King wrote in his book *On Writing*. Most of that book King wrote in 1997 before his near-fatal accident when a van struck him as he was walking on the side of a Maine road near his home. The rest of the book he wrote when he was struggling to live, survive through the pain, learn to walk, and attempt to write again. During his recovery, King wrote, "I have written because it fulfilled me."

Please try in this portion of your writing to feel that fulfillment by looking for what may be positive in your experience. Just as parenting programs suggest you catch your child being good to reward that behavior, catch the good in your story.

It was French literary genius Albert Camus who wrote, "In the depth of winter, I finally learned that within me there lay an invincible summer."

Find your own summer. Find the good in your history. Find the good in you.

Exercises

1. Go back to some of your earlier writing and ask yourself new questions. Was there something in the way you responded that was admirable, strong, or honorable? Was there something that happened just before or just after your Big Idea that you can write about fondly? Have you explored different roles other people played and did someone show you kindness or loyalty? Did someone help you?

2. Examine some of your motivations that could explain some of your behaviors and beliefs at the time. Were you hopeful or did you trust someone who did not deserve your trust? If so, write about the fact that you offered trust and how that is a good thing. Can you find the good in how you acted?

3. Write about specific good memories that may have run parallel to other events. Think back and describe pleasant feelings or fond recollections of a certain time and place. Add them to your story. Can you recall laughter? If so, write about that. Try to remember the good in your history so it doesn't all seem so rigid or narrow a view.

The winters in Chicago are unmistakably gray. And that's not necessarily a bad thing. In this essay that ran in the *Chicago Tribune* on January 18, 1998, I was writing about exactly the goal of this chapter: finding the good in the gray by seeking out the sunny side underneath. While some people like to talk about the weather and complain about it, I was trying to find what I loved about the pallor of winter. You can find the good in what you need to write about if you look deep enough.

A Gray Day Can Be a Great Day When You Color Your World

As usual for these January denouement days, it is gray outside. It is most always gray outside. I find it a reliable, reassuring constant that the sky is the color of a once-white T-shirt washed too many times, having taken too many tumbles in the dryer, perhaps with a pair of errant black socks.

But I love these days, these gray skies, the sun-is-gone days because—unlike most everyone I know who complains in that whiny tone about the sun never shining in winter—they are my novelist days. They feel so *Wuthering Heights*, so *Doctor Zhivago*, so Brontë sisters.

I know all about the reported effect of sunshine on people's personalities because I know (and intentionally avoid) people who appear grossly affected by its lack. And I seriously wonder why they bother. Mostly when friends harangue about the state of the soupy skies above, I ask, "Have you heard of 150-watt or, better yet, 200-watt light bulbs?" Turn them on all at once (which I did once when we lived in South Bend, Indiana, possibly the Midwest capital of gray). And when the electrician came to fix the fixture in the kitchen, which had burned through the ceiling that first winter, he advised me not to put two 200-watt bulbs in the same anything at once. I guess I got carried away.

Sure, it would be nice to have the sun Colorado-bright reflecting off the snow and actually need to wear the round black sunglasses I bought to look cool with my new leopard-print hat. But lamenting because the sky is gray and the sun has disappeared to somewhere far south and expensive to fly to is, to me, a phenomenally indulgent waste of time. At least none of us is stuck on Mir, where it is always dark and something critical and life supporting is broken. Again. Better to save the wailing for what matters—a paycheck arriving late, a friend who is hurt, a parent who is ill, or the children coming in the door in tears—than to feel burdened by the weighty color of the skies.

I was in Montana recently and the blueness of the heavens was humbling. It was a beautiful sight but so dwarfing that it doesn't take too long to understand why it is called big sky country. The broad foreverness of the azure was one kind of beauty, but there is a beauty, too, when the sky is gray and closes us in, with the heavens hovering down, zipping us in a worn, pastel mitten.

Still people complain, acting very Sylvia Plath. You've heard them, no doubt. "It's so gray here all the time," a man who lived in sunny southern California said to me at a party. "And this is significant to your life?" I wanted to respond, but didn't. I smiled and moved on to talk to a woman friend who would never dream of infusing the conversation with woeful tales of snow and freezing rain, let alone the regretful pallor of the sky.

So it's gray outside. So? I find I can get more done, work harder, and sleep sounder when not distracted by thoughts of outsidedness such as sledding with my boys, sun beaming on their faces. I feel calmer, contemplative, writerly. I'm not implying I don't welcome the days when it is so perfect and bright I feel grateful to breathe. I'm saying spending brain energy and emotions making an issue of things far out of our control—such as the gray that lingers above us from December to March—seems a silly way to spend a life.

I tell my friends who bring it up again and again that the grayness, too, will pass. It will be sunny and spring eventually, and without trying, we will get red cheeks and noses from watching baseball games and eating lunch outside.

I also remind myself that gray days are days without shadows, when the gray is even and equal, the milky wash spread generously and evenly over everything. It is these days heaven feels so close I hear its breath in my ear.

I tell them there are advantages to gray days. You don't have to squint. For several months you will have less wrinkle-producing sun damage to your skin no matter how bare you are. You can relax in the reliability that each day will offer the same pearly opaque, pale without exception, without interference, without surprise.

Still, I agree we do need bright color in our lives. So I boldly suggest you do as I do and wear fuchsia, yield-sign yellow, red, that bright celery green that is in every catalog folded into my mail slot, and the blue you wish the sky to be. I have a long fuchsia coat my mother gave me to wear a dozen years ago, and when I wear it, I feel instantly happier, having colorized my immediate landscape, like Ted Turner tinting the old black-and-white movies. I tell this to those people who find it impossible to shake what I understand has a title: seasonal affective disorder. So wear blush. And think of it another way. Think of your gray days as being under the dim glow of candlelight, the dimmer switch turned low to that flattering mystical near-darkness where everybody looks attractive.

chapter 17

Lessons Learned

By writing in this way, I am getting to know myself again.

—Leah, Writing to Save Your Life Workshop participant

The Moral of the Story

Oral histories, fables, and stories have been a way since the beginning of humanity's time on earth to find meaning in our dances of life. Each story-teller and each subsequent generation of storytellers could manipulate the story, pulling it and shaping its malleable form with his or her own style and sense of history. As a result, the stories changed shape and each story is never exactly the same story twice.

If you doubt that, listen to the family stories told at turkey-and-gravy-filled holidays by parents, grandparents, and children. You may even doubt they are the same story of the same event experienced by the same cast of characters.

By committing your story to paper, looking at it closely, examining both sides, and trying to honor your truth, you have escaped the amorphous tran-sience of oral history and made your story on paper immortal. The next step is to look at those words you have committed to paper. What lessons have you learned? What does this mean for you?

My boys love the book *Squids Will Be Squids* by the award-winning, megacreative children's book duo Jon Scieszka and Lane Smith. My children love it because the morals are witty, irreverent, and fresh, as in the tale of the Little Walrus, with the ending moral: "You should always tell the truth. But if your mom is out having the hair taken off her lip, you might want to forget a few of the details." They collapse laughing every time.

I'm not suggesting you go back to your words and add a snappy, one-line moral to your writing. I'm suggesting that we are all looking for the reasons and the justifications, the wisdom we can gather from our own experiences. If you look in your writing, you will find it is there.

In a National Public Radio interview I heard in fall 2000, author Tim Green was talking about writing. "Writing is calming for me," said Green, the author of several books including *The Letter of the Law*. He added, "It is a meditation."

The meditation of your writing can open you up for the possibility of further examining your story and seeing in it some lessons. For myself, I begin to see some of the lessons as I'm writing. Perhaps I see them only because I am writing down my experiences. Because I write every day and write what I am thinking and feeling as I am thinking it, sometimes I will understand a thought or an insight because I have written it, not ever having thought of it consciously before I started to write. It is new to me consciously and to the paper at the same time. I think, therefore I write. I write, therefore I think.

Put on Your Thinking Cap

Thinking and writing at the same time was called "composing at the typewriter" in journalism school. During my freshman year of college, I had a class called "Basic Writing," which was three hours long and required, a frightening and intimidating combination for a freshman. Students are in this class for three hours and produce a story—sometimes two—from information given in class. It's about deadlines, accuracy, and thinking on your feet. The instructors then weren't really trying to terrify us and make us switch to engineering or political science. They were trying to give us practice in a safe space.

Still, I remember the first class where we were to compose at our typewriters. In a basement classroom in Fisk Hall in September 1975, Julie sat in the back of the room, chain-smoking cigarettes, sniffling, and fidgeting back in the days when everybody seemed to smoke in class, including the instructors. Our instructor had just given us a fact sheet, and we were to write a news story from the facts. A few minutes into the assignment, it was obvious Julie was crying but trying to contain her tears. Occasionally she swore under her breath just loud enough for those of us around her to hear.

Many of us had written before; far too many were editors of their high school newspapers. But few of us had done that magical thinking at the keyboard on deadline, with the story due in forty-five minutes to be graded. To be counted toward a final grade. We could all write, sure. But so many of us had written everything on paper longhand before typing it. In this class there was no time to do anything but think and type at the same time. Type and think. Type as you think. Think as you type. Type. Think.

Julie started bawling louder. Eventually she got up and left the room. The instructor followed her into the hall, but not before Julie smoked about six or seven cigarettes and drank a Tab or two. And made us all feel as if we would do anything we could to avoid feeling the way she did. So the rest of us started to type and think at the same time silently. Eventually it became rote. Many of the students in the classroom that day went on to illustrious careers in journalism. Some of them swerved away from journalism. But we all made it through fine.

What's different for you from what Julie anguished over is there is no deadline for this. There is no grade here and no journalism degree hanging in the balance. So you have the luxury of writing and going back to think about it. Your story is not due in an hour. You can review your words and revisit your writing at your own pace to try to understand what it means. But don't let the words languish on the page, to be forgotten. Use them to make sense of the bigger picture.

Gaining Insight

What does your writing show you about you, who you were, how you experienced this, and how you view it now? Does the way you wrote, the manner of your writing, reflect how you were feeling?

Sometimes if what I am writing about is deeply affecting me, my writing is more staccato and truncated with shorter sentences and more pointed words. It is sharp, like my feelings. Is your writing more relaxed and lyrical, showing you that you have distance and context for the experience and can write about it feeling enough space to view it more intellectually? Is it so distant that you have been writing around your truth?

Trying to make sense of the content of your words does not mean that you are aiming to find a tidy, four-corner explanation or Aesop's fable moral. Whatever conclusions you draw are valid. Do you see your experience as random, a bit of luck and circumstance? Do you see your reaction and behavior as telling about who you were and who you are now? Does your writing help you to see a pattern?

"As I see my writing take on form, words create unspoken pictures. I see my emotions in three dimensions," says Iris, a friend and teacher.

We are all, I hope, aiming to live a contemplative life, one a few hierarchical steps above garden snakes. "I find my joy of living in the fierce and ruthless battles of life, and my pleasure comes from learning something," the Swedish playwright and novelist August Strindberg wrote in *Miss Julie* in 1888.

Let the writing help you learn something. Let the writing show you the insights you have culled and the wisdom you have gathered from your experience. Writing can be like an algebraic equation that seems like an indecipherable jumble of numbers and letters at first. But taken step-by-step, writing can get you to the answer you were searching to find, the solution to the puzzling equation.

"I write emotional algebra," Anaïs Nin wrote in 1946.

Is There a Happy Ending?

At book signings and events for my first book, there was usually a question-and-answer period when readers would ask me anything from the indignant to the compassionate. Aside from the occasional questions about sex, most often questions were about what I was doing now, and whether I was at peace. What I learned was that most people want to be assured of a happy ending. Somehow it makes them feel better and offers a cosmic justification that the world is a good, safe place. This guarantees for them that life hands out happy endings and that theirs is coming.

"Now that you have written this book, aren't you glad it turned out this way?" one well-meaning older woman asked me, her purse gripped in her lap.

Writing the truth is not compensation for the heartache and the sorrow. It does not overshadow the experience; it clarifies the experience and aids in the healing. Writing has made me feel triumphant in being able to articulate my story. Still, I would have rather not experienced any of it at all. I would have naturally preferred to be spared. But it all happened, and I chose to deal with it by writing. You are choosing to deal with your life in the same way I did.

Few of us escape life's bumps and grinds. If you doubt that, just read Charles Dickens or the metro section of your local newspaper. But it's not all bleak, and writing will help you to see that. Think of the character of Tiny Tim in Dickens's *A Christmas Carol*. He was perhaps the happiest character of all. You can write something profound about your experience of something painful. Writing is the alchemy that can transform your experience into something useful and instructive for you—so you can move on.

Writing Heals

After you have finished this book, written the exercises, and tried your best to tell your truth, I understand that all of a sudden you may not be awash with gratitude and relief for whatever section of your history you have explained to yourself. The lessons you learn may never overtake your experience and make you happy any of it occurred. But this experiment in writing may help you to heal one cell at a time. I know because writing my story helped me to heal.

The lessons I learned from writing my first book, *I Closed My Eyes*, about love, trust, control, and kindness helped me get to the base of my truth and get clear on where I stood in all the muck. It helped me because I coerced myself to be relentlessly honest in my writing. Without crippling my writing with the fear of judgment, I was able to write the truth to myself, more crucifyingly frank than I could tell the truth out loud to any of my sisters, brothers, friends, mother, or therapist.

I tried to write about it all with unselfconscious scrutiny until I could move past the tears, see the lessons that had to be learned, and attempt to master the lessons so nothing like that could happen again. The telling thing is I can go back and read some of those early chapters from my first book and still learn some new lessons about who I was then and who I was when I was writing it down. Even the tone of the writing tells me who I was and how much pain I was in. Had I not written about it with the goal of understanding the whole mess, I may still be crying, shaking my head, and wondering why. I would still be stuck in the sorrow and the anger.

This is why the writing has to move past just a chronicle of your history. You have to ask yourself why events happened. I'll wager that, looking back in your writing, you'll find the answers are there. You owe it to yourself to have this effort of writing be about something bigger than the account of the event itself. Take something away from it you can use, something that will help you grow.

What's the Point of It All?

During the weeks I was working on this chapter, the news on TV and in print was filled with the stunts of a young magician, David Blaine, who voluntarily encased himself in a block of ice for an ungodly sixty-one hours. This is not something the mother of young boys can watch idly, knowing that on my next business trip, my children may well try this at home in the backyard.

Not being a risk-taker, I was astounded by his inclination to do such a thing in the first place. And astounded as to why hundreds of reporters, cameras, and fans thronged New York's Times Square where ABC-TV was broadcasting his daredevil antics live. Were he trapped in an avalanche, I could see our national interest in extricating this innocent man overcome by nature's strength. He could emerge a hero, triumphant over his hostile environment.

But this was a grown man, a professional magician, who willfully and deliberately put himself at physical risk—even of death—for a publicity stunt. If the act was not orchestrated with TV cameras and crews, a man who deliberately harmed himself would be having a different sort of private recovery. And we would feel pity and compassion for him, not applaud him for his heroic endurance.

Of course I watched. It was the mother in me hoping he would come out in tears and say, "It was a dumb idea, kids, don't ever try anything this ridiculous." He came out of his icehouse weak, disoriented, and in obvious pain, exclaiming how much his feet hurt from standing in the ice for three days without boots or gloves. I'm telling you, this is every parent's nightmare.

Before he was sculpted into his ice block, Blaine told the camera that he would rather die in the middle of it than as a result of it. Is that the lesson he learned? Maybe the lesson the nation learned is that we were so sick of the 2000 presidential election recount that we would willingly watch some guy freeze himself nearly to death. On purpose.

You don't have to be buried in ice for three days to see there is a lesson to be learned from most anything and everything we do. But you do need to consciously look for the lesson.

Searching for Meaning

One Sunday afternoon, my friend Maxine and I enjoyed a late lunch, did some shopping, and were getting ready to head back to our homes. For these excursions, we meet geographically in the middle, each about fifteen miles from our houses, in a hip new strip mall. It's something we do a few times a year when our children are otherwise engaged.

Before we each drove our separate ways home, we stopped at a health-food store. Inside, near the entrance, a man and a woman were offering "free energy healing." Maxine is always game for that sort of thing.

"What's the difference?" she said. "How bad could it be?"

We both decided that we were not about to dismiss the opportunity to expunge some of the foul energy that just may well be infecting our auras. "What's there to lose?" she asked.

So we waited our turns. The woman in her gauzy purple dress and tightly wrapped bun and the man in his worn tweed blazer hitting above his wrists silently prayed, gestured, and dramatically swept the bad energy off a woman, who sat with her eyes closed just to the right of the produce department where the grape tomatoes and the ruby red grapefruits were on sale that week.

I snickered. When the other customer was finished, Maxine sat down, eyes closed as instructed. The man and woman told her to breathe deeply and went about exorcising her bad energy in exaggerated sweeping motions. I mumbled that her bad energy better not be falling onto me.

My turn was next. I tried to relax and let my judgments go. They made a comment about how I had a lot of bad energy around my neck, and because of their comments, I couldn't stop thinking about my neck. A few minutes later, they both breathed deeply and sent us on our way, but not before they handed us a typed sheet of paper with suggested donation amounts. So much for free healing.

Was it fake, a total put-on? Who knows? Maxine and I both said we felt better and more relaxed afterward. But we did close our eyes in a comfortable chair for ten minutes after a marvelous afternoon of friendship, camaraderie, and a delicious lunch of chopped salad. And it felt good.

Will the lessons you are looking for really be there or will you just be over-simplifying, trying to come up with a neat ending, laying down a simple moral to your life's story just to move on?

I'm not sure. But look for the lessons and you may find them. The lessons learned can be quite simple or they can be profound. But look in the writing when you are finished. Watch for lessons as you are writing. They will be there. Really, they will be there.

Exercises

1. Go back over your writing and read through it. Try to be relaxed and give yourself enough time and space—perhaps a half hour or up to several hours—when you can concentrate and be alone. Write down a list of questions on a separate sheet of paper. These can include questions about how you wrote your experiences and the effect those words have on you as you read them: Is your writing indicative of how you felt then? How do you feel when you read your writing now? What has changed for you?

2. Did rereading your writing help to clarify any points for you? Try to be objective, as if you are reading your writing as an account of someone else's life. Make a list on a sheet of paper with statements about the history you have written: "I was very young and didn't understand the consequences." "I was very hurt and my family didn't know because I didn't tell them." These are not blaming statements, just conclusions you can draw from reading.

3. Is there something you can see more clearly from what you omitted? Did you write your story without writing any words about your feelings? Can you comment about that? Did you write your story without including any participation from other people who were there? Is that significant?

4. When you look back on your writing, can you pinpoint what was easy and what was extremely difficult to put into words? It may be significant, for instance, that you could write pages and pages about your boss but could not write one paragraph about your father. Why did some of the writing seem to fall out of you, while other passages needed to be yanked? The way you wrote something and the ease or dis-ease of how the words came to you may be very telling and offer lessons for you to contemplate.

As a mother of school-age children, I end up sitting on buses a few times a year in the company of scores of other people's children for field trips to farms, museums, plays, or aquariums. I wrote this column for *West Suburban Living* magazine in September 1998. It's a funny look at how you can learn life lessons in the company of many nine-year-olds. It's also an example of how you can take any life experience and try to find some larger meaning in your writing.

A Third-Grade Field Trip

We were bumping along in the old yellow school bus going west on 290 headed to Aurora. In September, signing up as a chaperone for my oldest son's third-grade field trip to Blackberry Historical Farm Village seemed like a good idea, far enough away that it felt remote, non-threatening. I have since come to revise my notion of advance registration: Don't volunteer for anything you wouldn't want to do right now.

There we were without seat belts and with windows that didn't budge open: twenty-four uninhibited nine-year-olds, four mothers, one teacher, and a bus driver who didn't answer when spoken to. I learned at the end of that enlightening day that most of what you need to know in life can be learned on a third-grade field trip. It is the perfect scenario for life's lessons about control, love, commerce, work, simplicity, even ambition. Some of us have spent many good years acquiring this knowledge already; we just need to be reminded.

Lesson 1: You can't plan for everything. Take it from anyone who has ever scheduled an outdoor party only to greet the day with a monsoon, tornado warnings, or even snow: You just can't control the uncontrollable. As the early morning drizzle transformed into pelting, driving rain, those of us who relied on the sunny forecast and left the raincoats, umbrellas, and boots at home were left with wet hair, soaked clothes, and creaky rubber shoes, smelling like dogs who went for a dip in the Fox River. Life happens. Sometimes it pours.

Lesson 2: Love strikes when you least expect it. Who could have predicted that former lunchroom rivals would whisper to each other's best friends that they sort of, kind of, well, didn't really hate each other? To watch innocent love bloom at fifty-five miles per hour from across the ripped vinyl bus seats was reassuring. Only weeks before, Stephanie had stolen Jason's baseball cap and now, now, they were whispering about each other in a good way, confessing feelings that took courage to say out loud: "You don't really make me that sick." It was too romantic. Life can change in an instant. People can change. There are happy endings.

Lesson 3: Law of supply and demand. If everyone preorders one hot dog and if some of the students eat three hot dogs before the others find the picnic tables, there will not be enough hot dogs and more than enough crying, hungry children. "But Mrs. Griffin told me I could have seconds!" was one defeating defense to another child's screeching over a missed repast. You can't eat your neighbor's lunch and expect that the rest of the day will go smoothly. The other lesson is nobody eats the oatmeal cookies, so don't order them next year.

Lesson 4: Seek out specialists. A pair of earrings bought at a farm gift shop for 99¢ may just not make it off the bus intact. As a forlorn Blair discovered with her precious jewelry booty, a farm gift shop is not a fine jewelry store. It may be a good place to buy place mats or honey, but not jewelry. You wouldn't ask a jeweler to milk a cow, so why expect a farm to sell what they sell at Tiffany? Find the experts. Don't ask a dermatologist to set your broken leg and don't ask a plumber to repair your roof. Know who does what and follow the Yellow Pages.

Lesson 5: Success is relative. Some days all you can hope for in life is to get as many children back on the bus as got off the bus in the first place. Some days you just show up, write letters, return phone calls, and hope to eat lunch at your desk. Other days you can buy Microsoft, invent a cure for world hunger, and finish writing your novel. Still, on the days when all you can do is correctly count heads on the bus or make one person laugh, it is a good day.

Lesson 6: Keep life simple. All the high-maintenance, high-indulgence nine-year-olds survived a day without TV, Nintendo, soccer, computer games, and french fries. All watched entranced as the villagers made pottery, hammered horseshoes, and wove blankets on a loom. While I'm not suggesting any of us shut off the electricity and pretend we're Daniel Boone, keeping the twenty-first century temporarily at bay is not always a bad thing. The book *Simple Abundance* by Sarah Ban Breathnach was on the best-seller list for years. Maybe keeping life simple is a pretty good idea. Even if it's just for an afternoon that starts off on a bumpy old school bus.

chapter 18

Honor Your Story

*The words roam around in my head and my feelings give them
so many different meanings. It is only when I write the words down
do they become real experiences for me.*

—Lillian, teacher

Just Surrender

I was lying in the dentist's chair, my mouth propped open wide enough to
accommodate a top hat, and the hygienist—a kind, even-handed woman
named Pamela who calls me "sweetie"—was chiseling the plaque on my teeth
with a deafening electronic drill capable of dissolving the Washington
Monument into fine dust.

Earlier when she had asked my preference, I had chosen the old Bing
Crosby and Danny Kaye movie *White Christmas* to supply distraction during
my prolonged cleaning session. After all, it had been five years since my last
appointment. It really only seemed like two. The white plastic TV was sus-
pended from the ceiling, but the large, rectangular light she used to see past
my gums and into my brain blocked a third of the screen at times.

Breathing through my nose, I was trying to concentrate on the movie and ignore the pounding in my chest and the hydraulic drilling to my back teeth, all of them plagued with antiquated fillings that needed to be replaced at the cost of a semester of college tuition. I was also mildly amused by the absurdity of this 1940s classic movie—the impromptu dance numbers, the forced dialogue, the costumes, the cheeky innuendoes—and me straining to see it all out of one eye as I flinched and shuddered with each molar-poking eternity.

But for the moment, or the hour, or the hour and a half, all I could do was surrender and be there. I had no choice but to live through this part of the story, watching *White Christmas* and planning the chapter I would write, the e-mails I would return, and the dinner I would concoct for me and the boys that night. It was solace that I knew whatever transpired in that black vinyl chair, I could write about it later—if I wanted to write about it later. So I let my shoulders loosen and relinquished the death grip on the Kleenex I was shredding on my lap with both hands.

Embracing Both the Good and Bad

Whatever happens in your life, you have the right to write about it, whenever you want to write about it. It's a freeing thought. It may even help you get through some of it. From the dentist appointments to the events that are bigger than we ever imagined, we can write about it all.

We get through so much of our lives because we have to, because it is required. The regular doctors' appointments, the children's earaches, the symposium where the speaker goes on about two hours too long, the six loads of laundry from the family vacation, the grade school reunions, the emergency room waiting areas, the flat tires on the expressway, the award dinners where you don't win or they mangle your name if you do. And the flu.

But there is a whole lot more of life: that perfect cup of coffee, the afternoon at the beach, the friendship that has lasted decades, the soul mate who understands us perfectly, the siblings, the book that touched us deeply and made us laugh, the song that made us dance. Sometimes what we have lived through is momentous and its impact on us life altering. Sometimes what feels insignificant as it happens actually changes who we become.

The greatest news is we can write about it all, the joyful parts as well as the painful parts. The small triumphs, the enormous hurts. And we can honor ourselves and our truths in our own words, anytime, anyplace. We can write to save our lives just because we dare to. You need no official permission slip, authorization code, or PIN number to access your words. Your story is there for your taking. Take it, write it, and honor it.

If you think you need official permission, here: I give it to you.

Author and memoirist Annie Dillard wrote in *The Writing Life*: "One of the few things I know about writing is this: Spend it all, shoot it, play it, all, right away, every time. Anything you do not give freely and abundantly becomes lost to you. You open your safe and find ashes."

Write about it so your life is not lost, none of it is lost.

Because writing has helped me sand the jagged edges of my life, I have been suggesting you spend time—the amount of time is your choice—writing about your life. Do so because it is healing, entertaining, and illuminating and will teach you things you did not know about yourself before you started to write.

It's All There

Writing what is inside of you is like playing the Ouija board game where your hand guides the game piece to the letters that spell out the response to your question. There is no mysterious force or evil spirit giving you answers, in spite of what transpires in the early moments of the movie *The Exorcist*. You had the answers all along. You are controlling the Ouija board, no matter how insistent any fifth-grade girl in the early morning hours of a slumber party can be. You are writing what is already inside of you. You are in control of your words. You just need to go down and retrieve them from the well. But they are there. Go down and get them.

The act of writing will teach you about how you think and feel and remember, what you remember and why, not because the writing is coming from some source outside of you, but precisely because the writing is coming from a place deep within you. It is perhaps the first time you accessed your own wisdom and put into words your own interpretations or account of your history. It is the cheapest form of therapy I can imagine.

Whether you have been writing to preserve a story you were afraid to confront or writing to keep alive the joy of an event or phase, saving it matters. Your words about it matter. Your story is absolutely worth saving. That you tell your story and how you tell it are critical to understanding yourself, and will help you to keep healing and growing.

Your Writing Has Impact

"Writing does not exclude the full life, it demands it," wrote Katherine Anne Porter, who began publishing her short stories and essays in the 1930s.

Your story matters.

This has been a story for you to tell yourself. Stories have always been a way for us to tell ourselves truths. The Bible is an astounding and elaborate collection of transcribed stories: oral histories, family legends, songs, inspirations, prayers, letters, dictations, even parables created to tell stories with Big Ideas that were much larger and profoundly more far-reaching than the metaphors used. Ancient Greek and Roman mythology contains stories people told themselves to explain a mysterious world. *The Canterbury Tales* chronicles stories of men and women in the Middle Ages. The diary of Anne Frank, one of the most influential works of literature in the twentieth century, is a collection of the written, private thoughts of a young girl. Leslie Marmon Silko, an author of Native American descent, once said, "It's stories that make this a community."

Your story is important. By writing it down and committing your truth to paper, you have honored your life, your truth, and who you are in the world.

"I am going to write because I cannot help it," wrote Charlotte Brontë, the nineteenth-century author of *Jane Eyre*, a fictionalized account of her own experiences, which revolutionized modern literature with its daring romance and feminism.

"I shall feel bad if I do not write and I shall write bad if I do not live," wrote Françoise Sagan in 1956.

Writing accompanies living. Writing is not meant to supplant the living, nor even to distract you from the living of your life. Writing is meant as an underlining illumination; a written, conscious clarification; an affirmation of your life. It is meant to serve as punctuation to a life, an accessory to a wardrobe of experiences. If you think of your writing as reward, as an honoring of yourself, you will approach each writing session without fear or anxiety, but with a sense of entitled relief. It is my hope for you that you are convinced your life's stories deserve commemoration and that writing is the way to that end.

One marvelously talented student, Vivian, in a Writing to Save Your Life Workshop, keeps me updated on her writing. She wrote to me recently that she can divide her life into "BW," or before workshop, and "AW," or after workshop. It's flattering and her talent is stunning. But all I really did was give her permission to tell her story and convince her that it matters. And she believed me.

Tell your story because it matters. And the reason I care that you tell the story is because it gives us all permission to tell ours. Author Julia Cameron, in her *Reflections on the Artist's Way* audiotapes, talks about the underground reservoir of talent and creative energy that we can all tap at will. I like that image. Beneath us and around us is a wealth of support, a deep river or ocean of permission allowing us, urging us, to tell our stories to ourselves, or to others, because our stories do matter. Your act of writing to save your life gives me the impetus to keep writing to save my own.

You Are Never Too Young to Tell Your Story

I was at a cocktail party recently that had a familiar script. I was standing by the makeshift bar in the kitchen and a professorial man with graying hair, clear blue eyes, and a black turtleneck started a conversation. He told me he was a computer scientist by day, percussionist by night, but that he really wanted to be a writer. I told him I was a writer and we talked a little about creativity and swapped some names of great writing books that were helpful to each of us.

Then he started to bristle and asked me all the predictable questions people do when you tell them you're a writer: Where was I published? What newspapers and magazines do I write for? Is my book actually in bookstores? Then he asked me to tell him about my first book. I gave a one-sentence synopsis saying it was a creative nonfiction memoir and he clipped, "But aren't you too young to write a memoir?"

Maybe he was just trying to compliment me about being younger than he was, but I responded that if you are old enough to have memories and can hold a pencil you are old enough to write a memoir. He got all rigid after that and moved on to talk to a woman in a black leather skirt standing by the artichoke dip—the warm version with fresh Parmesan, bread crumbs, and sliced, toasted almonds, not the old-fashioned one with mayonnaise and the processed Parmesan cheese that comes in the green can.

As my sister Maureen would say, "Oh well."

I don't know how old you are, but whatever age you are, I assure you that you're old enough to write your story. If you can read this book, you can write. If you can write words on paper, you can write the stories inside you that need to be told and need to be written.

Saving Your Life in Words

An author friend of mine, Anne McCracken, is a fine journalist and a thoughtful, lyrical writer. She co-wrote and co-edited the book *A Broken Heart Still Beats* following the death of her young son in an automobile accident. When I asked her to tell me about how writing has helped her honor her story and move through life, she wrote me this:

> In tough times, I've taken many long, solitary walks. Because they help. When, like Mark Twain, I too wondered how I could live once my child did not, friends would offer to walk with me. But mostly I turned them down—for I knew I would not be alone. Like house-bound hounds, Pain, Anger, and Despair were clamoring for my attention.
>
> Ever at my feet, nudging me with their noses, barking their noisy, insistent barks, the trio refused to be ignored. And in the end, even if one made me rage or cry, I've never been sorry that I walked them.
>
> For me, personal writing works much the same way. I usually turn to

my journal in desperate urgency, overwhelmed by emotions. The words race out at first, then slow to a dawdle. I don't plan to show my journal to anyone, yet I write as carefully as if I do. I agonize over just the right words. I scratch out sentences. I rewrite. And I've learned, like Julian Barnes's widower in *Flaubert's Parrot*, how terribly inadequate the language of emotions is. "The words aren't the right ones; or rather, the right words don't exist."

It's a hard mental workout, this forcing order into my chaotic thoughts. But like most exercise, it does feel good. The restless hounds and I have taken yet another walk. Because it helps.

She's right. The writing helps.

You've done quite a big thing writing about yourself and your life. You've saved what needed to be saved, so you can look back on it as a tangible account of where you have been.

Like photographs from a vacation, some snapshots will be candid and out of focus, some will be flattering and posed with the perfect lighting, well focused with balanced composition. But whatever the snapshot is, together the roll of pictures produce for you an account of what it was like at just that place, at just that time, and it will be yours to keep. You were really there. It really happened that way. You saved your life in words. That's really something.

Exercises

1. It's time to celebrate and honor yourself for daring to write about your own life. I am suggesting a real ceremony. The when, where, and how of it is totally up to you. Whether you want to read your work out loud to yourself in the mirror or you just want to silently look through your writing with a cup of your favorite tea beside you, you need to perform a miniritual. You can light a candle or make for yourself a magnificent meal and set the table elaborately with your favorite plate, silverware, and small vase of flowers.

2. Make yourself a memento to celebrate and honor your story. You may want to write in calligraphy the words *My story matters* or even *I honor the truth in me*. What seems fitting to you is the right combination of words; it could even be the first sentence of your story. You can type these words on a computer in a font that seems festive and print it out on marbleized paper. Frame your declaration and place it near your desk on a wall or on a table to remind you that your truth is sacred and that you have succeeded in honoring your story in words.

3. Continue to listen to your truth and the truth of others. Be a source of calm and encouragement for people you encounter. Knowing what writing the truth has done for you, when someone tells you a story, just listen. Resist the urge to be judgmental or to ask how and why their story is true or how they dare to tell it in words. Whenever someone tells you a story they know to be true, offer the healing and uplifting affirmation "I believe you."

I wrote this essay that I later read many times during speeches to women's groups. It is about honoring your truth and honoring the sanctity of true friendship. Do you know someone who honors your truth unconditionally?

I am lucky enough to have several close friends who do. But I didn't have the courage to tell my truth—about who I had become in my marriage—to my close friend Dana, a roommate in college. She and I had drifted apart after graduation and then back together again. I wrote about how that felt, why I allowed myself to float away from this anchoring friendship, and why I needed to tether myself to her friendship again and remain honest about who I was.

She is someone who will always honor my story as I will always honor hers. Perhaps you are lucky enough to have a friend who will do the same. Before I could seek the solace of her friendship, I needed to honor my own story. Just as you need to honor your own story for yourself. In your writing, you are that trusted friend.

Flying to Los Angeles Alone

I flew to Los Angeles alone. I took the window seat, used both arm-rests, and lingered over magazines, the ones with the quizzes about your emotional or nutritional health. I ate all the peanuts offered and rented the movie. I walked to the bathroom alone and closed the door behind me. Click.

Once we landed, I carried only my bag filled only with my things—all of them impossibly impractical. She was not there in the terminal waiting, of course. She is always late. But I knew she would come.

Taking two days for myself was an outrageous prospect for a mother of three small children: my youngest was nine months old and newly weaned, my middle son was three, and my oldest had just turned six. But I was going to the wedding of another friend in Los Angeles and I hadn't seen Dana, my best friend from college, for five years. The last time was when I flew to Los Angeles on a business trip, taking my oldest son with me, my only son at the time. The three of us went to the beach and Johnny Rockets where Dana taught Weldon, who was one, to sip through a straw.

There wasn't much to separate us then, only the miles and one small little boy. We were both so full of hope. The memories of being so young together were still vivid. We talked for hours at a time, and took several rolls of film—both of us here, both of us there; you stand there, while I shoot. I didn't tell her everything, but I told her enough.

When she finally did arrive, pulling up outside the baggage claim at LAX, I remembered when I first saw her that September afternoon, almost twenty years ago, in room 203 of the Northwestern University student apartments on Orrington Avenue, across the street from the old hotel. We were assigned to be roommates, along with two other women. But it was Dana, the girl from Scarsdale, New York, with the dark brown hair and the hazel eyes who would be my best friend. She would be the friend who would change me and change with me as we grew older and grew together, grew up and grew apart. I felt about her the way I felt about my three sisters, adhered to each other with a closeness that was assumed, respected, revered.

For three of our four years of college, we shared dorm rooms and apartments, changing the cast of other roommates each year. I was the writer. She was the actress. I helped her with her lines for the university plays and once she got me a very small part as an extra in a made-for-TV movie starring Robert Conrad where she was one of the leads. I was a pregnant hillbilly wearing a flesh-colored belly pad under my coat. I was on screen for as long as it took the flatbed truck I was sitting in with a half dozen other extras to drive across a street. She read my stories in the campus newspaper all school year and in the magazines I wrote for in the summers. We talked about our plans—to be rich and famous and wildly successful—and never once did we think the other foolhardy.

Dana was imprinted on me the way only a good friend can be at a time in your life when anything seems possible. We cried together, laughed together, told our secrets to each other and no one else. Partners can pass in and out of your life, I learned, but it is a tireless friend who clings to your soul. It is with these other women friends that you perfect the art and science of being a woman, from learning how to French braid your hair to how to draw on all the talents within you.

Before anyone else outside my family, it was Dana who let me speak my dreams without question. She told me to say out loud each day into the mirror what I dreamed of doing with my life. She told me to claim it. "I want to be a writer," I said. And we listened to each other, calmly and without a hint of criticism or derision, full of faith and acceptance, our friendship born of trust and upheld by time.

She was my closest ally at a time in my life when I was laying the foundation for who I am now. We were only practicing back then at being grown up, coaching each other through every rehearsal, catching each other when we would fall. But the practices helped us through the live performances years later.

The years passed after college graduation, with Dana in Los Angeles and me in Chicago, then later Dallas, South Bend, and back to Chicago. Our friendship was forced to become abbreviated, and though I no longer knew what she did every day, I always knew what she meant to do.

For a few years, I took my annual vacations from work to see her, and she flew to see me, more than once, with a fresh heartbreak. I watched her in the roles she landed on TV shows and in movies. Once on a business trip to Des Moines, I turned on the TV and saw her in a feature film on the hotel's movie channel. I laughed out loud and called her immediately. I got her answering machine.

Seven years after college I married a man I had known my entire life. Dana was a bridesmaid of course, and looked radiant in the pale mauve dress with the white lace standing alongside my sisters and sisters-in-law. She rode with us in the limousine to the reception at the Union League Club downtown. She came to visit us once, and we called each other on our birthdays and half-birthdays; my birthday is June 5, hers is December 5. And oftentimes on the phone she told me my voice sounded strange.

We no longer spoke all that often, but when we did, we spoke well. Without elaborating much, I told her my life did not feel as good as it looked and it was not as I had planned. But years passed and each of my children was born. They were consuming, distracting, and glorious. She asked to speak to them all on the phone, even if all they did was gurgle. I talked less about my husband because she asked a lot of questions I didn't want him to overhear me answer.

She stopped acting and became a teacher of English as a second language. She learned to play golf. She fell in love with a kind man whose name she said differently than any other man's name I had heard her say. She later got married. I helped her get ready, rode with her in the limousine to her wedding, and toasted her at the reception. And when we talked to each other on the phone, I always pictured what she looked like and I always remembered that here, here is a true friend, one who knows who I am and who I planned to be. Here is someone who believes in me.

Nine years after I was married, I admitted the truth to her about my marriage. Only then was I able to hear the intuited words she had begun asking me a half dozen years before, "Why are you still married to him?" I had never told her all, but she said she knew by what I didn't say. She flew to see me and the boys on that first Thanksgiving I was separated. It was her first long break from school. She played with the boys and talked to me, listened to me. When I needed her, she was there. Eating cold pizza from the refrigerator, playing cards with my sons, and helping me reclaim my dreams.

Like a balloon, she was full of encouragement, light as helium, holding me up, not letting me go. She is a friend I needed, the friend I always need. Someone who will honor my story. Someone who will wait for me to tell it, knowing before I can even incite the courage to tell it to myself.

chapter 19

Enjoy the Music in You

Having survived, a healing process begins and I write no longer from fear but with relief, compassion, acceptance, and a desire to validate both my endurance and the resulting insights and growth.

—France, Writing to Save Your Life Workshop participant

Applause!

In the syllabi for the classes I teach at Northwestern and on the blackboard of my Writing to Save Your Life workshops, I write one of my favorite quotes: "To love what you do and feel that it matters, how can anything be more fun?" Katharine Graham, the author and businesswoman who steered the helm of the *Washington Post* for decades, said it and lived by it.

It is joyful to write when you believe what you are writing matters. I have been urging you to invest in the sanctity of your story so you do enjoy the writing—the process as well as the result. Get a kick out of yourself for doing it. Applaud your efforts. Applaud your writing. Enjoy the idea that you are one of the storytellers. It is important to record your story and tell it even if you are the only one who will ever read it or hear it.

Loving the Writing Process

At Saint Luke's School in River Forest, Illinois, where I attended first through fourth grades, there was always a miraculous someone chosen to be the audio-visual helper. Before videotapes, there was the clumsy, green-gray, steel reel-to-reel projector. It needed to be threaded painstakingly and, of course, wheeled down the hall to the proper classroom before and after the movie.

I thought to be chosen as AV helper was to be declared near sainthood, a step above priest and a notch below martyr. As AV helper, you missed a few minutes of class going to retrieve the projector from one classroom, then a few minutes more delivering it to the next classroom or returning it to the dark closet with the oversized mops and ancient buckets. I was gravely jealous of the AV helper, especially if there was a test.

Coming and going at will is a concept that was anathema in Catholic schools, so the only person above the status quo who was never questioned in that arena was the AV helper. Most often a boy, most often bespectacled, most often the best at math, he possessed the magical gift of being able to turn on the projector after loading the film. When there was a snafu, he was called to fiddle with the sound buttons and rethread a wayward loop of film, as if he were one of Christ's chosen soldiers. It was always a task beyond the comprehension of the black-and-white-habited nuns, who fumbled at all prospects mechanical, but who could diagram a sentence at whim. Sometimes if the AV helper failed, the nun brought in the grumbling janitor who had sprinkled so many floors with sawdust in his time that he permanently lost all sense of humor.

Being able to write down your experiences makes you special in the way an AV helper was thirty-five years ago. With your writing, you can come and go in your past. You can conjure the words you need to say and write them down to save them and your feelings. Whenever and wherever you wish to do it.

"I love writing the way some men love women," author and journalist Rick Bragg wrote in his captivating memoir of his Southern upbringing and exceptional writing career, *All Over but the Shoutin'*.

I love the writing too. I urge you to try to love the writing. Love the process and the result because the writing is yours and you have written the truth. For me writing is not just a way to make a living, pay the taxes, and keep the boys in soccer shoes, blue jeans, and video games. It is a way to enjoy my life. If I didn't write for a living, I would find a way to write anyway. I would write in my spare time. I would work to write if I couldn't write for work.

"To write is to create a space for myself to heal," says my friend Linda Berger, a teacher and mother of two sons.

Writing this book was a gift for myself and a way to express my joy in the craft and the boundless possibilities of growth and healing afforded you when you place your thoughts on paper. Being able to declare what I know and feel about writing and sharing it all in these pages has been a delightful journey.

I get a kick out of it because it's a euphoric plateau I can reach just by typing what is in my head and in my heart. I love the writing because it is one way I define myself; for that I am grateful. I can always write, no matter how old I am, no matter what I look like, no matter what others do or say.

More than forty years ago, novelist and essayist Flannery O'Connor wrote: "I certainly am glad you like the stories because I feel it's not bad I like them so much. The truth is I like them better than anybody and I read them over and over and laugh and laugh, then get embarrassed when I remember it was I who wrote them." O'Connor devoted herself to her writing and creating acclaimed short stories and novels while she suffered from lupus, a crippling disease that claimed her life in 1964 when she was thirty-nine years old.

For me, I not only like my stories, but the act of writing evokes a feeling of mastery, just as on that day when you're five years old, and for the very first time, you're riding on the two-wheeler without a pair of clumsy training wheels and you really do feel as if you're flying. Honest-to-goodness airborne.

Oh, What a Feeling

It's that same feeling as when you read the words that you have won the big sweepstakes. It's the feeling when you're standing outside in a snow-silenced morning and the sky is that Magic Marker blue so brilliant it seems fake. It's the feeling you have when you answer the phone to a voice you haven't heard in years. It's the genuine hug that gives you chills.

Writing can afford a fulfillment not only in observing the result of your writing in well-crafted sentences and paragraphs but also in the active participation. It's the same joy of actively doing that you get from hanging the garland over the front door just right, putting together a bookcase, flipping an egg and placing it gingerly on the plate without the yolk breaking, or swimming twenty laps and loving every stroke.

Once you gain that momentum in your writing, it seems as if you dissolve your marriage to time and place; there are only the words with you and you are in charge of them. It was hard for me to get to that zone in a crowded, noisy newsroom. It's much easier to get to when I am in my home office, the boys are at school, and the house is quiet and still.

You can get there by using the tools in this book and by allowing yourself the room to enjoy the process of writing, opening the door and viewing the writing not as an assignment but as a playful, sacred endeavor. Know that you can get there.

Writing is not the sole territory of an exclusive club of writers fiercely protecting the secret password and handshake. It's a club with open, rolling admission. And if you want to write, you can join. So write. Not only is the writing free, it is freeing.

In his book *How to Write*, Pulitzer Prize–winning author Richard Rhodes writes: "Writing was the answer for me. Somewhere within me I seem to have known that. If you want to write, you may feel that writing is the answer for you as well."

In this book, I have been suggesting that writing can be an answer for you to heal and save your life. As it begs the questions, it contains the answers. It may open you up to what you may not have pondered before, and it may sensitize you to look at the world more fully. "Writing is the soul's expression of the heart," says Maria, a mother and friend.

Consider It a Dialogue

Writing to save your life is not a new concept, but I hope this book has presented the idea to you in a new, accessible way, one that is empowering and enriching. By including in these chapters the insights of talented writers over the centuries, contemporary writers, and perhaps people like you who have just begun to write, I warmly invite you to validate your own wisdom and join the dialogue. "When I listen with my hands, my heart hears better," says Mary, another writer friend.

Almost a century ago, poet Ella Wheeler Wilcox wrote in her poem "The Word":

> You may choose your word like a connoisseur
> And polish it up with art.
> But the word that sways, and stirs and stays,
> Is the word that comes from the heart.

Allow your words to come from your heart. It is the best starting point.

Looking Inside

I have been writing since I was a kid. Professionally, I have been writing for exactly half of my life. To make a living and build a career, I have written about celebrities, footwear, fast food, and advertising, even beer, art, and movies. I have written about books, fashion, trends, companies, politics, and my own life. In all those years, I have spent thousands, maybe millions of words on paper or blinking computer screen, and because of it, I have grown to understand what I think and how I feel.

Writing has taught me to see outside of me as well as inside of me.

Mine is an ongoing narrative that is fluid and peaceful at times, comfortable in the way of old gardening shoes or a soft chenille bathrobe. At other times the writing is choppy and confronting, full of missteps and self-doubt, in the same way looking at a brochure in a foreign language makes you wonder how you will ever understand it. Eventually you look up the meanings of the words and can understand the message.

Novelist Kurt Vonnegut, who in 2001 began his two-year tenure as state author for New York, told a reporter from the *Albany Times Union* that writing was healing for him as he recuperated from a fire that nearly claimed his life.

The seventy-eight-year-old author of such classics as *Slaughterhouse-Five* and *Mother Night* told reporter Doug Blackburn, "Everybody should write to find out who they are and where they are." He added, "Right now, though, I'm thinking I want to turn my typewriter into a musical instrument because I can really play it."

Think of your writing as a song you get to play. Enjoy the music of your words.

The words can be like a bulb you plant in your garden in late fall to see bloom in the spring, poking through the dark ground. Or your words can be like an amaryllis bulb—round, brown, and awkward, looking like a turnip— that you plant indoors in November, hoping the flowers will be tall and bursting in color for the holidays. Your words are the bulbs you plant, water carefully, and hope will flower and show you a way to heal.

Some call this a life review. Some call it a journey to the self. I call it scribotherapy. Whatever its name, writing is one way I have found to maneuver through the waters of life. The writing uncovers what is there; it does not create something that was not there before the writing began. The lookout crew on the RMS *Titanic* did not create the iceberg; the iceberg was there all along. What you need to write about is there too, and whatever you discover in your writing was there before you gave it words. You are only claiming the truth, dealing with it in your own words, and hoping to heal as a result. You are going somewhere with the light of your pen, hoping to see in the darkness.

"Follow your inner moonlight," poet Allen Ginsberg said in an interview with Michael Schumacher in *On Being a Writer*. That inner moonlight will illuminate the path for you to find the words you will need to write your story.

Believing in Yourself

Driving home from Evanston recently I was listening to a National Public Radio piece about the seventy-fifth anniversary of the release of Hoagy Carmichael's classic song "Stardust." The composer of the celebrated American jazz songs "Georgia on My Mind" and "Up the Lazy River," Carmichael had told a reporter in an earlier interview that he almost lost the song forever because he composed it in his head without writing it down right away.

He explained to the interviewer that about six weeks after he was fiddling with the original tune on the piano as a college student in Indiana, his good friend asked him about it. Hoagy had forgotten about the melody, but his friend played it on the piano from memory and told him he needed to write it down because it was so good. So he did. The song was so much a part of who he was that the first book in Carmichael's two-volume autobiography published in 1946 was called *The Stardust Road*. The almost-forgotten "Stardust" is a magical, timeless song that has been recorded more than two thousand times in the twentieth century.

Believe that your truth is a beautiful, original song you need to write down so it will not be lost. You have music and stories inside of you. You owe it to yourself to honor and remember them. Write them down. And get a kick out of yourself for being able to do it at all.

In the extraordinary book *Free Play*, violinist, artist, and author Stephen Nachmanovitch writes: "There is a place in our body to which we can turn and listen. If we go there and become quiet, we start to bring the music up." He is writing about imagination and the creation of our own truths in music and writing.

Bring up your own music. Let the words swell, rise, and come out from within you, resonating your truth in your own original song. Trust in the glorious energy and power of your own words. Own what you write and own what you feel. You will find that you will write what you need to write and excavate the details you need to preserve. Keep the writing for yourself, a testament to your strength and your ability to articulate your story. And in the process of writing your truth, you will heal yourself and save the life you need to save.

Enjoy a life that celebrates the hallowed words dancing within you.

Exercises

1. Write ten reasons why or how your writing has felt good to you. You can write that you began by learning to explain past events or using your words constructively for your own healing. You can simply write that you enjoyed the quiet time of writing. You may write that you have learned how good you are at expressing your thoughts and feelings. You may write that you are the only person who knows this truth and your writing has saved your truth from being lost. You may want to say that reading your writing shows you how intelligent, creative, sensitive, and insightful you are. You can also write that writing helps you remember. Be sure to read the list out loud and congratulate yourself on each point.

2. Write on a piece of paper: "I am writing to save my life so I can heal." Place that in your wallet, on a mirror where you can see it daily, or on the side of your computer. Read it aloud to affirm your mission to record your thoughts and feelings and that your ultimate goal is to heal. Know that you are writing in order to grow and move past events that shadow you, not live in the past. If you feel overwhelmed by any of it, please seek outside help from a therapist, clergy member, friend, or relative.

3. Make a list of how your writing has helped you begin the healing process. You may even notice physical results of the writing; you may be sleeping better after writing or you feel an overall sense of relief after reading what you have written. If it is the case, write that your insights gathered from your writing have helped you take steps to mend friendships and family relationships or alter your behavior or attitudes. The healing may be as simple as a renewed boost to your self-esteem. Keep checking with yourself about how the writing is working for you and what some of the positive results are. Some of the benefits may not be immediate, but may evolve and grow over time. Good luck and good writing.

I was driving with the volume turned up, a Madonna tape playing in the cassette deck. I was shoulder-dancing and singing to myself as I made my way through traffic. I glanced in the rearview mirror to see the swirling lights of a police car behind me. I pulled over and waited. The officer came to my window and said, "Lady, do you know how long I have been behind you? You have to turn the music down and pay attention." He was pulling me over for an expired sticker and gave me a warning about paying attention. Truth was, I really don't know how long he had been behind me.

I can get lost when I listen to music I love. You can get absorbed in the music of your writing. This is an essay I wrote in the fall of 1996 that ran in the *Chicago Tribune*. It's about a radio station I wish existed. But it is also about enjoying the music in your own story, the music in the words you write to save your life.

WSHE in Chicago

I have this fantasy. I am driving in the car—alone—and I am listening to the radio and every song that plays is exactly what I want to hear, whether it is Mariah Carey or Roberta Flack. The deejay is this really funny, smart woman who doesn't sound as if she has been up all night smoking cigarettes and pounding shots of tequila. And then the commercials come on and even those are interesting. They're about seminars or spas far away and not one, not one single one of them is about a weight-loss program or dating service.

And then on this station, WSHE, the news announcer comes on and it's this woman's crisp voice and all the news is about women changing laws, saving lives, running companies, having babies, or having just some of all of it. No one is yelling. There are no jokes about breasts or blonds. Occasionally there's commentary from women writers, and I laugh and I try to remember the names of the books they quote so I can send them to my closest friends. Alice Walker reads chapters from her books. I feel understood.

But mostly I want to listen to the station because of the girl songs. It's the ladies singing into the microphone who get to me. I've been in this phase for the last few years. It is not out of some conscious decision to block out all the male pop tunes of the 1990s and before. It comes out of a natural inclination as I get older and grow to be more sure of who I am that the wisdom, the sanity, and the pure, soothing quality of the girl singers is all I really want to hear. That includes girl country singers, Broadway divas, even Barbra Streisand and Bette Midler singing themes from stupid movies.

And when I say "girl," it isn't to demean or to describe a preadolescent female. I say it fondly, out of reverence for who we have all been. A girl is a female, all females, a woman, a grandmother, a nun, all of us who can at some level, at some point, from some soul quadrant be the girls we once were: telling secrets, sharing truths, belting one out in the bathroom, the high notes drowned out by the shower. Aretha Franklin is a girl. Tina Turner is a girl. Annie Lennox is a girl. Madonna is a girl.

Please don't think I have always been transfixed by popular music. Mostly I don't know or even recognize the names of the artists on the Billboard top 10. I was never the kind in high school who walked around with the lyrics to "Stairway to Heaven" handwritten in a notebook, painstakingly transcribed after starting and stopping the album 165 times to get every word and syllable right. It's not that my life is so devoid of definition that I need a total stranger with a decent falsetto to offer me some contrived explanation for my moods. I don't need a constant soundtrack for my life.

It's a release. In the rare moments I do something for myself, I find a beautiful, nurturing voice with lyrics I can respect as different, or identify with completely, as comforting as an aural hug.

I would rather hear Bonnie Raitt than Hootie and the Blowfish any day of the week.

Just as did every girl growing up in America in the 1960s, I lip-synched into a hairbrush along with Diana Ross. But I also had a

Rolling Stones phase. I was devoured by a deep craving for anything Mick Jagger and also listened to Led Zeppelin so loud and so blaring over and over again. I also had the capacity to listen to the same song twenty-eight times in a row. I loved Paul McCartney, being totally convinced for at least a decade that he sang "Michelle" only to me, even though he spelled my name wrong.

That was an era in my life, those teen years, when I was afraid to be all that I was. I spent most of my high school years presenting myself as two different people, with two opposite sets of friends. I had my friends in the honor classes who were great for study groups, but usually fairly dull on the weekends, and my other friends from homeroom and gym who mostly skipped classes but were a lot more fun. My parents didn't like that group much, but they had great stories to tell on Mondays.

While a part of me was trying on prom dresses and swooning in the mirror accepting the Academy Award listening to Dionne Warwick or Martha and the Vandellas, another side of me was sitting in the basement wasting time to the loud thuds of heavy-metal bands. Eventually I came to my senses, in time for college where I learned you could be smart and still have fun. And for the first time, I heard Bonnie Raitt in concert. I haven't liked the boy bands and heavy rock and roll since, although I still think Sting is cute and that Michael Bolton would not be bad company on a desert island. Even without the baseball cap.

I'm not afraid to be me anymore.

So in my dream I'm in my car driving alone and I'm not lost. The radio is playing WSHE. And it's a girl song. It can be opera, it can be jazz, it can be the blues like no man has ever sung the blues before. I am singing with her and tapping my left hand on the side of the car, or playing the air keyboard with my right. She's singing loud and I hear her, really hear her. No matter who she is, she is a girl just like me.

Afterword

Thank you for daring to write your story. I am interested to know your comments about writing and whether the exercises in this book have helped you to begin the process of healing. I applaud you.

Contact me by e-mail at michele.weldon@hazelden.org. Or contact me by regular mail:

Michele Weldon
P.O. Box 5721
River Forest, IL 60305

Recommended Reading

Barrington, Judith. *Writing the Memoir: From Truth to Art*. Portland, Oreg.: Eighth Mountain Press, 1997.

Berg, Elizabeth. *Escaping into the Open: The Art of Writing True*. New York: HarperCollins, 1999.

Best American Essays, The. New York: Houghton Mifflin, new edition published each year.

Bradbury, Ray. *Zen in the Art of Writing: Releasing the Creative Genius within You*. New York: Bantam, 1990.

Bragg, Rick. *All Over but the Shoutin'*. New York: Pantheon, 1998.

Brande, Dorothea. *Becoming a Writer*. New York: Putnam, 1934.

Cameron, Julia. *The Right to Write: An Invitation and Initiation into the Writing Life*. New York: Tarcher, 1998.

Capote, Truman. *Music for Chameleons*. New York: Random House, 1975.

Chancellor, John, and Walter R. Mears. *The New News Business: A Guide to Writing and Reporting*. New York: Harper, 1995.

DeSalvo, Louise. *Writing as a Way of Healing: How Telling Our Stories Transforms Our Lives*. New York: Harper, 1999.

Dillard, Annie. *The Writing Life*. New York: HarperCollins, 1998.

Edgarian, Carol, and Tom Jenks, eds. *The Writer's Life: Intimate Thoughts on Work, Love, Inspiration, and Fame from the Diaries of the World's Great Writers*. New York: Vintage Books, 1997.

Fontaine, André. *The Art of Writing Nonfiction*. New York: Thomas Crowell, 1974.

Fredette, Jean M., ed. *Writer's Digest Handbook of Magazine Article Writing*. Cincinnati, Ohio: Writer's Digest Books, 1989.

Frey, James N. *The Key: How to Write Damn Good Fiction Using the Power of Myth*. New York: St. Martin's Press, 2000.

Friedman, Bonnie. *Writing Past Dark: Envy, Fear, Distraction, and Other Dilemmas in the Writer's Life*. New York: Harper, 1994.

Gerard, Philip. *Creative Nonfiction: Researching and Crafting Stories of Real Life*. Cincinnati, Ohio: Story Press, 1996.

Gilbert, Sandra M., and Susan Gubar, eds. *The Norton Anthology of Literature by Women*. New York: Norton, 1985.

Goldberg, Natalie. *Thunder and Lightning: Cracking Open the Writer's Craft*. New York: Bantam, 2000.

———. *Wild Mind: Living the Writer's Life*. New York: Bantam, 1990.

———. *Writing Down the Bones: Freeing the Writer Within*. Boston: Shambhala, 1986.

Golub, Marcia. *I'd Rather Be Writing*. Cincinnati, Ohio: Writer's Digest Books, 1999.

Greene, Elaine, ed. *Thoughts of Home: Reflections on Families, Home, and Homelands*. New York: Hearst, 1995.

Heffron, Jack. *The Writer's Idea Book: How to Develop Great Ideas for Fiction, Nonfiction, Poetry, and Screenplays*. Cincinnati, Ohio: Writer's Digest Books, 2000.

———, ed. *The Best Writing on Writing*. Cincinnati, Ohio: Story Press, 1994.

Higgins, George V. *On Writing: Advice for Those Who Want to Publish (or Would Like To)*. New York: Henry Holt, 1990.

Johnson, Alexandra. *Leaving a Trace: On Keeping a Journal*. New York: Little, Brown, 2001.

Keyes, Ralph. *The Courage to Write: How Writers Transcend Fear*. New York: Henry Holt, 1996.

Kilpatrick, James. *The Writer's Art*. Kansas City, Mo.: Andrews McMeel, 1984.

King, Stephen. *On Writing: A Memoir of the Craft*. New York: Scribner, 2000.

Kipfer, Barbara Ann. *The Writer's Digest Flip Dictionary*. Cincinnati, Ohio: Writer's Digest Books, 2000.

Klauser, Henriette Anne. *Writing on Both Sides of the Brain: Breakthrough Techniques for People Who Write*. New York: HarperCollins, 1987.

Kriegel, Leonard. *Flying Solo: Reimagining Manhood, Courage, and Loss*. Boston: Beacon Press, 1998.

Lamott, Anne. *Bird by Bird: Some Instructions on Writing and Life*. New York: Anchor Books, 1994.

———. *Traveling Mercies: Some Thoughts on Faith*. New York: Pantheon, 1999.

Maisel, Eric. *Living the Writer's Life: A Complete Self-Help Guide*. New York: Watson-Guptill Publications, 1999.

Mandelbaum, Paul, ed. *First Words: Earliest Writing from Twenty-two Favorite Contemporary Authors*. Chapel Hill, N.C.: Algonquin, 1993.

McClanahan, Rebecca. *Word Painting: A Guide to Writing More Descriptively*. Cincinnati, Ohio: Writer's Digest Books, 1999.

McMeekin, Gail. *The Twelve Secrets of Highly Creative Women: A Portable Mentor*. Berkeley, Calif.: Conari Press, 2000.

Mee, Susie, ed. *Downhome: An Anthology of Southern Women Writers*. San Diego, Calif.: Harcourt Brace, 1995.

Nachmanovitch, Stephen. *Free Play: The Power of Improvisation in Life and the Arts*. New York: Tarcher/Putnam, 1990.

O'Conner, Patricia T. *Words Fail Me: What Everyone Who Writes Should Know about Writing*. San Diego, Calif.: Harcourt Brace, 1999.

Parker, Dorothy. *The Portable Dorothy Parker*. New York: Viking, 1973.

Perry, Susan K. *Writing in Flow: Keys to Enhanced Creativity*. Cincinnati, Ohio: Writer's Digest Books, 1999.

Plimpton, George, ed. *Writers at Work*. New York: Penguin, 1985.

Ramsland, Katherine. *Bliss: Writing to Find Your True Self*. Cincinnati, Ohio: Walking Stick Press, 2000.

Rhodes, Richard. *How to Write: Advice and Reflections*. New York: Quill, 1995.

Roorbach, Bill. *Writing Life Stories: How to Make Memories into Memoirs, Ideas into Essays, and Life into Literature*. Cincinnati, Ohio: Story Press, 1998.

Schneider, Myra, and John Killick. *Writing for Self-Discovery: A Personal Approach to Creative Writing*. Boston: Element Books, 1998.

Sims, Norman, ed. *The Literary Journalists: The New Art of Personal Reportage*. New York: Ballantine, 1984.

Sims, Norman, and Mark Kramer, eds. *Literary Journalism: A New Collection of the Best American Nonfiction*. New York: Ballantine, 1995.

Spotts, Carle B. *Ideas and Patterns for Writing*. New York: Holt, Rinehart, Winston, 1967.

Steinberg, Sybil, ed. *Writing for Your Life #2*. Wainscott, N.Y.: Pushcart, 1995.

Strickland, Bill, ed. *On Being a Writer: Advice and Inspiration . . .* Cincinnati, Ohio: Writer's Digest Books, 1989.

Ueland, Brenda. *If You Want to Write: A Book about Art, Independence, and Spirit*. Saint Paul, Minn.: Graywolf Press, 1987.

Walton, Todd, and Mindy Toomay. *The Writer's Path: A Workbook to Release Your Creative Flow*. Berkeley, Calif.: Ten Speed Press, 2000.

Welty, Eudora. *One Writer's Beginnings*. Boston: Harvard, 1983.

Winik, Marion. *Telling: Confessions, Concessions, and Other Flashes of Light*. New York: Vintage, 1995.

Wolfe, Tom. *Hooking Up*. New York: Farrar Strauss Giroux, 2000.

———. *The Right Stuff*. New York: Farrar Strauss Giroux, 1979.

Writer's Digest Guide to Good Writing, The. Cincinnati, Ohio: Writer's Digest Books, 1994.

Zinsser, William. *On Writing Well*. New York: Harper, 1980.

———, ed. *Inventing the Truth: The Art and Craft of Memoir*. New York: Warner, 1998.

About the Author

An award-winning journalist for more than two decades, Michele Weldon writes regularly for the *Chicago Tribune* and her work has appeared in hundreds of major newspapers and national magazines. Her first book, *I Closed My Eyes,* has been translated into French, Spanish, and Dutch. In 2000, Weldon earned the International Women's Peacepower Media Award for nonfiction as well as the Individual Courage Award from Rainbow House in Chicago.

Her work has appeared in two anthologies, *Joyce Carol Oates: Conversations with Joyce Carol Oates* in 1989 and *Belly Laughs and Babies* in 1997. Weldon has appeared as a guest on TV shows on NBC, ABC, and BBC as well as on several local network and national cable stations. She has been a featured guest on more than ninety radio stations across the country and in Canada.

She is a lecturer at her alma mater, the Medill School of Journalism at Northwestern University, where she has taught at the graduate and under-graduate levels since 1996. Weldon gives Writing to Save Your Life workshops in Chicago and around the country and is a frequent keynote speaker to local and national groups.

Living in the Chicago area with her three sons, Weldon serves on the board of directors of Sarah's Inn, a domestic violence services agency in Oak Park, Illinois, and is a member of Children's Memorial Guild, a fund-raising arm of the medical center. She is a member of the Journalism and Women Symposium as well as the Association for Women Journalists.